MANAS
NATIONAL PARK

RED RIVER
An imprint of LBS Publications

LBS Publications
Registered office: LBS Centre, Panbazar, Guwahati – 781 001,
Assam, India
Branch Office: 20, Ansari Road, New Delhi - 110 002, India
World Wide Web: www.lbsbooks.com

First Published in India in Red River by LBS Publications 2007

© Photographs: Dushyant Parasher
   Text and Design: LBS Publications
International rights: LBS Publications

RED RIVER™ and NATURE HERITAGE SERIES™
are Trademarks of LBS Publications

ISBN 81- 85921-18-0

Photographs and Design by Dushyant Parasher
Published by Bhaskar Dutta Baruah,
LBS Publications

Printed and Bound in India

Cover: A r
Asiatic wa
seen in the
near Math

Half title
rare sight
most of th

Title doub

Nature Heritage Series™

MANAS
NATIONAL PARK
A PICTORIAL HANDBOOK

SIVASISH THAKUR

PHOTOGRAPHS
DUSHYANT PARASHER

RED RIVER

Cradle of nature—In Manas National Park plant life can be seen taking root in the most unexpected places

About Nature Heritage Series

Nature is the cradle of all life forms on earth. Successive generations of living beings have inherited nature in one state and handed it down to the next, in another. It is well known that lately we have not been very kind and understanding to the very environment and resources that have not only sustained us, but have also allowed our industrial and economic progress this far. A lot has been lost in the past, but mercifully not all. We still have some hot-spots that represent the original pristine beauty of Mother Nature. This remaining heritage needs our immediate attention and understanding.

MANAS National Park—our first pictorial handbook in the Nature Heritage Series™— is a step in that direction. These books will show the beauty of land, its fauna, flora and people; provide information on history, geology and eco-systems; highlight concerns and suggest solutions. They will be a traveller's guide, a nature lover's companion and a handy source for policy planners.

Red River™ Nature Heritage Series™ is mandated to showcase Nature Heritage, and this heritage knows no boundaries, regional, national or international. LBS would be happy to hear from serious nature writers and photographers from around the world, who think they can add more titles to this series.

Publisher
bdbaruah@lbsbooks.com

Indian roller—These otherwise ordinary-looking birds display a fascinating spectacle of their colourful underwings during flight.

CONTENTS

Above and following four double spreads: Pristine forests of Manas are extremly rich in fascinating plant and insect life.

Preface

MANAS

Somebody once said of Manas that Earth must have looked like it before man set his foot on the planet. Nothing can be a better description of or a more fitting tribute to the magnificent Manas, which is a manifestation of Nature in her unblemished self. Combining in itself pristine forests, breathtaking scenery, and a bewildering variety of wildlife and flora—a rare occurrence

Garden of nature—A beautiful water body on way to Daimari from Kokilabari in the eastern part of Manas.

Pod of a wild jasmine bursts into a colourful display of flashy red. It is one of nature's way of protecting seeds from birds who usually avoid vegetation and insects of red colour, taking them to be poisonous.

Manas is home to a very large variety of insect life
yet to be fully studied and recorded.

Sand castles on the river bed—a fascinating example of insect architecture in Manas.

anywhere on Earth—Manas is indeed a paradise. A night's stay at the quaint forest bungalow at Mathanguri, the most preferred tourist spot in Manas, can be as exhilarating an experience as one can hope to get in any jungle. With the roar

Above: This juvenile pied hornbill was seen around the picturesque forest bungalow at Mathanguri.

Top: The forest bungalow at Mathanguri.

of the gushing Manas which bifurcates into two sparkling blue channels just below the bungalow atop the hillock, and the vast expanses of the Bhutan hills providing the backdrop, it is a true Eden where you can feel your senses opening up to the loveliness and wonders of the world of nature. On a moonlit night that bathes the forest in a faint glow, or on a night when the moon plays hide and seek with the dark clouds, as you sit on the balcony of the bungalow, feeling the cool breeze soothe your senses and listening to the roar of the fast-flowing Manas, you are elevated to a different plane altogether — far, far away from the stress and strain of the daily grind. Spending some time here is sure to give you an ethereal feeling, making you realise that nature appeals through the eye of man to his inner spirit –– the spirit that, to quote Wordsworth, 'rolls through all things'.

Early morning next day, as you roll your eyes over the breathtaking scenery unfolding before you along the riverside, or take a stroll down the narrow jungle road, or even venture into the dew-dipped woods, you will be overcome with a feeling of both awe and admiration, probably emanating from your initiation to the mysterious and powerful ways of nature. Chances of encountering animals in their natural environment are also very much a possibility in the morning hours. While you are sure to see deer or even bump into a solitary gaur, if you are lucky and know where to look, you can get a passing glimpse of the majestic tiger, the 'large-hearted gentleman of the Indian jungles', as immortalised by Corbett. Nothing can equal the sight of a tiger in the wild, which makes it so special and the cynosure of the questing eyes of all wildlife tourists.

There are so many ways to relax and unwind yourself in Manas. You can just sit before the icy blue waters of the Manas river and savour every bit of the out-of-this-world landscape. You can take a boat and drift downstream, feasting your eyes on the scenery on both banks. In fact, taking a boat ride is also

Icy blue Manas river flows next to the forest bungalow at Mathanguri.

one of the best ways to view wildlife in Manas. As you leisurely pass the enchanting jungles, an inquisitive gaze from the buffaloes grazing on the bank would greet you. You may also come surprisingly close to a herd of elephants frolicking in the water. Early morning and evening is the time when most animals come to the river and the innumerable jungle streams to have a drink, and with luck on your side, you can get to see many of them. Birdlife in plenty is also what you

A group of beautiful Green bee-eaters.

are sure to come across, even if you miss out on some of the more exciting but reticent animals. It is not for nothing that Manas is called a bird watchers' paradise, and the beautiful winged denizens of the jungle will never disappoint you. It is guaranteed you will encounter peacocks almost everywhere, with flocks of up to 50 at places. The highly-endangered Bengal florican is another major resident of Manas, as are the swamp francolin and the Finn's baya.

A view of Manas river from the Bhutan border near Mathanguri.

Elephant rides apart, which is the best and safest way to have a firsthand account of the dense, forbidding jungles of Manas and its inhabitants, trekking is an exciting option that the enthusiastic traveller would love to try out at Mathanguri. There are a couple of well-laid-out trails that trekkers can use. With the Forest Department's permission, one can also cross over to the Bhutan side (the Royal Manas National Park) by just wading through the river, which

A walkway in wilderness—with permission from the forest department, it is possible to explore some areas of Manas on foot.

remains shallow at many points during the dry winter. The beautifully-decorated summer palace of the King of Bhutan is another attraction. Surrounded by virgin jungles, and with troupes of the rare golden langur making it their favourite jaunt, the palace presents a lovely sight.

Above and top right: Golden langur—This blonde-haired langur of Manas region, was first photographed by the famous naturalist EP Gee, in 1953. In 1955 this new species was officially named Presbytis geei—*Gee's langur.*

Above: A Barred owlet
Top: Wild flowers

Chapter 1

A NIGHT IN THE JUNGLE

The night was dark, cold and cloudy, punctured occasionally by the faint rays of the waning moon that played hide and seek with the shadowy patches of haze looming menacingly over the horizon. The dim glow of the moon lent a rather eerie touch to the jungle. The forest was silent, except for the rustling of leaves in the wind, the occasional sound of the

Grasslands interspersed with Simul trees present a tranquil picture of Manas at dusk.

cricket and the shrill cry of some night bird, which served to heighten the haunting effect. A thin veil of mist originating from the wind-swept Bhutan hills draped the woods, restricting visibility. At times the heavy overgrowth made it impossible for the moonlight to penetrate it. And when it did, where the jungle was relatively sparse, it presented a haunting spectacle, with the foliage of the trees silhouetted against the moon. The huge trees that seemed to shoot right

A green fortress—The impregnable forest.

up to the sky stood tall and firm as eternal sentinels guarding the sacred woods, looking dark and foreboding. For the uninitiated who had little experience of jungle life, especially in the night, it was enough to put his nerves under strain. It is strange how one's senses start playing all sorts of tricks whenever one's dependence on the eyes loses relevance on a dark night in a dense forest. The tree becomes an elephant, motionless and staring. You hear a rustling

sound and jump and turn back, only to discover that it was no tiger, crouching and ready to pounce upon you from behind—just an abrupt gush of wind against the swerving branches and leaves.

All of a sudden, the silence of the jungle was shattered by the deafening roar of a tiger —and this time it was for real. The king of the jungle was not very near, though, but its roar was enough to unnerve the inexperienced juvenile elephants, which trumpeted in panic and ran helterskelter, trying to break away from the safari. Only the huge bull elephant, Lachit, on which I was riding along with Abhijit Rabha, the Field Director of Manas and the mahout, remained totally unfazed and continued with his regal, no-nonsense trudge. Raising his heavy trunk occasionally to scent the air, he seemed little bothered about the tiger. But the young elephants were quite unsettled for a while, and

Heavy undergrowth and overhanging creepers, a typical view in the deep forest.

the riders had a tough time clinging on to their backs, as they dashed through the dense woods full of entangling creepers, climbers and overhanging branches. The Ranger, Mohan Chandra Brahma, was hit by an overhanging branch, and fell off his elephant. Being a strapping, athletic person, Brahma did not suffer any injury, and soon rode the elephant again. Gradually, all the upset elephants settled down and started to move in a row. The calm and stately demeanour of Lachit, too, probably had a soothing effect on the young elephants. It seemed Lachit had indeed stood up to his name (Lachit Borphukan was the most acclaimed Assamese general, who handed the all-conquering Mughals a crushing defeat at the famous Battle of Saraighat in 1671).

It was after several decades that the Manas authorities embarked on such a long ride on elephant back. The main purpose, of course, was patrolling. And we were fortunate that for the first time, people other than those from the Forest Department were part of the team which consisted of eleven elephants and about a dozen forest personnel, the mahouts and three — four journalists, besides Bansbari Ranger Brahma and Field Director Rabha.

Earlier, after a sound night's sleep at the pleasantly old-fashioned forest bungalow overlooking the gorgeous Manas river at Mathanguri, we had set off in the morning for Giyati at Bansbari, the starting point of our much-awaited safari. From there we moved eastwards. Kokilabari, towards the far east of the park, was our final destination. I have always

A profusion of ferns gives Manas a very 'Amazonian' look.

been fond of elephant rides — not just because it is the best way to observe wildlife but because I find it a rather relaxing exercise. And it fascinated me no end to watch the elephant as the gentle giant trudged along calmly, nonchalantly, making its own way out of the thick foliage and feeding from the leafy boughs as it walked, without bothering to stop.

It had rained in the night, and the jungle, bathed in the early morning sun, looked simply

Behind this lush green facade lies a world of wild animals, birds and insects waiting to be explored.

stunning. It was a riot of gleaming green everywhere. Drenched in rain, the foliage glowed like emerald. The excited chirping of beautiful birds and the flapping of butterflies of every possible hue, added to the splendour of the captivating forest. We did not, however, see a lot of animals, especially from close range, as we were passing through dense woods most of the time. The noise from such a big procession of elephants also made the denizens of the

jungle retire deeper into the forests. Probably it was us — the trespassers and violators of the blissful tranquility of the jungle — who were watched indignantly by the animals from their 'safe' abodes. However, we did come across deer, wild boar, elephants and gaurs. We were disappointed at not encountering the large herds of buffaloes normally associated with Manas, though we met a solitary bull and a couple of straying adolescents here and there. Then there

Malayan giant squirrel

were the acrobats of the trees, the capped langurs, who emitted animated sounds and made faces at their distant cousins passing below. Birds we saw in large numbers, often encountering large congregations of magnificent peacocks for which Manas is rightfully famous. We were also lucky to witness a couple of peacocks engrossed in their most graceful 'courtship dance' to woo their ladyloves. Spreading their enormous spans of colourful

Capped langur

plumage as far as they could, the magnificent birds presented a remarkable sight. A couple of Bengal floricans, a highly-endangered species, also made a brief appearance, as did the Pallas' fishing eagle. But the tiger, the most sought-after animal of the Indian forests, continued to elude us. Claw marks on trees, pug marks on sandy riverbeds and a deep-throated roar were the nearest we came to the presence of the lord of the jungle. The dry beds of several jungle streams and rivulets made for interesting observation. The spoor on the dry sand indicated the presence of a variety of animals, and in good numbers too, as we stood examining the trails for a long time.

But the most important sighting, which only I could make among the whole entourage, was that of a rhino. Rhinos were thought to be completely wiped out (although there had been unconfirmed claims of the existence of one or

A leopard's tell-tale pug marks on the river bed in Manas.

two) during the decade-long period of social unrest in the area during the 1990s. I could see the rhino only for a few seconds before it melted into the woods without a sound. This was very significant because it was the first time that a rhino had been sighted in Manas in years.

More excitement was in store for us. Never in my wildest dreams did I think that I would be encountering a gang of poachers right inside the forest. But that is what actually happened, as I stood witness to a gun battle between the poachers/tree-fellers and forest guards. After several hours of riding, as we were approaching the Daimari beat, we stumbled upon a hideout of poachers and tree-fellers. A few rounds were shot from either side, but seeing that they were outnumbered, the miscreants took to their heels after a few minutes, leaving their booty behind. There was a trail of destruction of forest wealth, with felled trees and cut-down stumps spread

Many such beautiful streams crisscross Manas National Park.

Rhino—A rare glimpse.

across a large area. Tell-tale marks were everywhere, that laid bare the wounds inflicted on the forest. There were wooden planks smoothly cut from the felled timber. A large number of axes, hacksaws, and other equipment used to fell trees besides wooden *thelas* (push-carts) also lay scattered. The camps even had kitchen appliances and utensils, and hot rice was steaming from a few containers. As our bellies were burning with hunger, having ridden for

Gradually descending landscape of Manas National Park as seen from Daimari camp on the Bhutan border.

several hours after a light breakfast, we gleefully helped ourselves to the food that seemed rather mouth-watering at that moment. It was apparent the gang was used to staying for days inside the jungle and must have been carrying on with their depredations for at least a week. There was still sufficient ration for several days. Blankets, warm garments and combs were among many other things seized. No animal carcass or body part, however, was found.

It saddened me when I thought of what we were making of this most vibrant wilderness and a world heritage site. It was obvious that the timber smugglers were receiving help from the local villagers, as the *thelas* carrying the timber had to go through the village routes. Probably it is time these people were made active participants in the conservation process, failing which there seems to be little hope for Manas.

As we continued with our ride, the jungle never ceased to excite us through its varied ambience and settings. The forests changed to wearing different looks as we entered different territories. We passed over large tracts of grassland, patches of semi-evergreen forest and areas of mixed deciduous forest; waded through small swamps, crossed innumerable jungle streams and climbed up steep inclines.

Then, after a few more hours of ride, dusk set in slowly, and before we realised it, it was

Sunset at Manas.

already night. It is always so in the Indian jungles — after the setting sun heralds the evening, it takes only a while for darkness to descend and envelope the jungle in its fold — quietly and unnoticed.

As we tried to come to terms with the darkness that had put a black shroud over the surroundings, a grim realisation hit us — we were lost. We were supposed to cover the journey in about six to seven hours, but we seemed nowhere near our destination even after ten hours. Even the mahouts and forest guards were at a loss as to which direction to take, and their arguments amongst themselves only added to the confusion and tension. For some time we drifted in different directions. It was 9.30 p.m. and still there was no sign of any end to the forest, which looked more mystifying and ominous in the night. Then, at long last, we heard signals made by a 'rescue team' coming

This reed grass can grow up to a height of 4-5 metre.

from the Kokilabari side, which was our destination. When we finally reached the camp, it was almost 11 p.m. For a while we could hardly walk after getting down from the elephants, our limbs completely stiffened by the long, arduous ride. However, the rousing welcome given to us by the waiting members of the NGO, Maozigendri Eastern Manas Eco-Tourism Society, and the sumptuous feast that followed, were enough to make us forget our fatigue and exhaustion to a great extent.

Headquarters of Manas Maozigendri Ecotourism Society at Kokilabari.

The safari was an extremely rewarding never-to-be-repeated experience for us in more ways than one. It enabled us to observe and marvel at the forest, its varied life forms and amazing biodiversity from close quarters. It was the first time I had personally visited this wonderful forest, but the memory of this first visit and the bond that I developed with Manas, will surely last my whole life, if not beyond.

Above: A wild elephant disappearing into the misty folds of forest.
Top: A Spotted dove.

Chapter 2

THE LEGEND OF MANAS

Steeped in mystery and secrecy, the vast, unknown, and unexplored wilds of Manas have always evoked a sense of fear and foreboding among humans. The result is that a number of myths and legends have come to be intrinsically associated with the place. In fact, the fables and tales woven around it have had such a profound influence on the psyche of the locals that these

have become very much part of the folklore. From days of old, the eerie jungles of Manas, which even the sun's rays cannot penetrate, have stirred the onlooker's imagination with awe and fascination, something that explains the wealth of myths and spooky tales surrounding Manas. The sheer number and the diversity of wildlife in Manas have also been the stuff of folklore and legends. People, especially old-timers, still recount tales of coming across thousands of

Grassland and forest cover—An ideal elephant habitat.

buffaloes, deer and elephants in the forbidden jungles of Manas long before it became a protected area.

One such enduring saga relates to the 'Daughter of Manas', a lady in white who is generally revered as the protective deity of the forest and whom some people even claim to have actually seen. She is invariably associated with a big herd of wild elephants, which is said to be under her command. To some others, she is a

human being with supernatural powers —— someone who was raised in the jungles of Manas. Even today, people narrate tales of catching a fleeting glimpse of the phantom figure of a lady in a white robe, who moves swiftly with the grace of trees swaying in the wind, and melts into the jungle before one can even recover from the shock. So deep-rooted and widespread is the belief that a full-length Assamese feature film, *Manas Kanya* (Daughter of Manas) was made on the theme.

Among those who claim to have seen the mysterious lady of Manas is the late Kumud Chandra Choudhury, a renowned hunter and elephant-catcher, who had a long association with Manas in the 1960s when hunting was still in vogue. Says his wife Renu Choudhury: 'My husband used to stay in Manas for long periods in connection with hunting and elephant-capturing expeditions. And he invariably used to recount his experiences to us, although I was not much interested in those initially. But I remember him telling me how he had, on more than one occasion, come across a lady wearing a one-piece white cloth. Always amidst or nearby a herd of elephants, she was known as *pagli* (the mad one) and the herd as *pagli sahan* (*sahan* means a herd of elephants). It was also generally believed that her blessings were essential for meeting with success in capturing elephants, and many shikaris used to offer puja (ritual seeking divine blessings) to her before venturing into catching elephants. Sometimes she was also seen sitting on a tree while the elephants grazed.'

According to her husband, says Renu

Choudhury, the lady in white was a real human being who must have been brought up in the jungles.

'Once, my husband was able to approach her from quite near but his efforts at starting a conversation did not succeed, as she probably did not understand any human language. He had also offered her some food, which she did not take,' she adds.

Mysterious indeed are the ways of Manas. People say that on dark, moonless nights, burning earthen lamps can be seen floating down the Manas. No one knows from where these lamps come.

The origin of the word Manas (generally called *manah* in Assamese) is quite interesting, and there are several accounts behind it. One version seeks to attribute the origin of Manas to the goddess, Manasa, the deity of snakes, who is also the daughter of Lord Shiva, the destroyer of evil. Legend has it that many, many moons ago, there was once an invasion by dreadful snakes (much in the manner Hamlin was invaded by rats) on the human habitations within the vicinity of the forests, killing and driving people out. Finding no other way to contain the furious assault of snakes, the harrowed people approached Goddess Manasa to rid them of the menace. In order to please the goddess and earn her blessings, a cave at Matharguri (Mathanguri on the Assam–Bhutan border) was dedicated to the worship of the deity, and people flocked to it to pay obeisance to her. The devotion of the people pleased the goddess, who is ill-reputed for her notoriously hot temper, and she cured the snake-bitten people and liberated the snake-infested area. From then onwards, the jungles came to be known as Manas and the same name was given to the river that passed by the cave and through the forests.

There is another interesting legend about the origin of the name *manah*. Thousands of years ago, when there was neither the river nor the forest, there lived a youth by the name of Manah at Matharguri village. He was alone except for his mother, and was the apple of her eye. Manah, a handsome young man, fell in love with a lovely maiden, Nayantara. Their love, however, was in danger of never getting fulfilled, as the prevalent social customs came in the way of their marriage. Manah was from a low caste while his paramour belonged to a higher caste. Finding no alternative, they decided to tie the knot in the village temple, with the goddess as witness. The priest of the temple, who was a revered as well as feared figure for his supernatural powers, was also known to fulfil the wishes of those who pleased him. It so happened that one dark night the love-struck couple arrived at the temple, took a pledge in front of the goddess to remain united forever and sought the blessings of the goddess and the priest. Trouble, however, started after the priest, Bhriguraj, set his sight on Nayantara, a lady of exceptional beauty. The devil entered the priest's head and he lost his mind. He sent Manah on an errand under the pretext of fetching something necessary for the rituals of their marriage, drugged Nayantara and fulfilled his carnal desire on her. When Manah returned, he saw the priest lying with an unconscious Nayantara by his side. He realised everything and his anger knew no bounds. With the machete that was used for sacrificing animals in the temple, he beheaded both the priest and Nayantara, and surrendered before the people. Then followed a trial, which sentenced him to death. All the appeals of his poor mother, who cried and cried till she could cry no more, fell on deaf ears and Manah was put to death in a cruel manner. The mother was completely shattered and resolved to kill herself by banging her head at the altar of the stone-hearted goddess, who had failed to heed her prayers to save her only son. Her bid to end her life moved even the goddess, and a deafening thunder was heard in the sky. Somewhere in the misty mountains of Bhutan, a peak collapsed and a huge volume of water gushed out with great force, sweeping everything that came in front of the terrifying torrent. Such was the force of

The roar of Manas river is linked with many local legends.

the current that it swept away the temple, the body of the evil priest, and the whole village. The body of Manah was also carried away by the surging waters and his mother ran along the river shouting 'Manah, Manah'. Her heart-rending shrieks were echoed in the river that also roared 'Manah, Manah'. And from then onwards the river and the surrounding jungles came to be known as Manah. People say that even today, the roaring waters of Manas at Mathanguri reverberate with the pitiful cry of the mother for her beloved son.

Another line of thinking attempts to relate the origin of the word Manah to the invasion of Assam by the marauding Maans (settlers from Burma), who defeated the ruling Ahoms and plundered the State several times in the 17th century. It is said that the Maans, who entered Assam from the east, could advance to the west

Manas—A vibrant wilderness with a backdrop of Bhutan hills.

as far as Manas but not beyond it. The word Manah has been formed out of two words — *Maan* and *Aah* (a verb meaning 'to come'), signifying that the Maans had come up to Manah during that period. It is generally believed that the advancing invaders did not deem it fit to cross the forbidden jungles of Manas.

Celebrated as the abode of tigers, elephants, rhinos, buffaloes, gaurs and as many as five species of deer, Manas came to symbolise the most vibrant wilderness in the State. People still recount with wonder and fascination the astounding animal wealth of Manas. Although sometimes it may seem a bit exaggerated, it is a tribute to the bounty bestowed on Manas by Mother Nature.

Above: Manas as seen from the northern boundary near Daimari.
Top: Sunset from the edge of the forest at Kokilabari.

Chapter 3

BOUNDARIES AND RIVERS

Among the oldest protected areas in the State, Manas has a long history of conservation. It used to constitute, and still constitutes, a part of the largest conservation area in the region with contiguous forests in Bhutan in the north and Buxa Tiger Reserve of West Bengal in the west. The Sonkosh river in the Kokrajhar district marks its official boundary in the west. Towards the

east, Manas Tiger Reserve extends up to the Dhansiri river in the district of Darrang. The total east-west length of the Tiger Reserve extends to 230 km.

The conservation process of Manas began during the days of British rule in India. The British were quick to realise the importance of protecting these virgin forests, and Manas was accorded the position of Proposed Reserve Forest (PRF) as early as 1905. It became a Reserve Forest

A Large cormorant waiting for breakfast.

(RF) in 1907 and in 1928 it was upgraded to a Game Sanctuary, covering an area of 360 sq km (Manas and North Kamrup RFs). It was declared a Wildlife Sanctuary in 1950 and then its area was further extended to 391.02 sq km in 1955. In spite of its importance as a global biodiversity hotspot, Manas had to wait for several decades to attain the status of National Park in 1990. Its area was enhanced to 519.77 sq km with the addition of Panbari, Kahitama and Kokilabari

Reserve Forests.

A prime tiger habitat that harboured the country's second highest concentration of the great cat till the late 1980s, Manas was covered under Project Tiger immediately after the project was launched in 1973. Then, as a tribute to its outstanding universal value, it was recognised as a world heritage site in 1985. Manas added yet another feather to its cap when, in view of its pristine natural eco-system representing the overall biota of the region, it was honoured with the title of Biosphere Reserve in 1989 under the UNESCO's Man and Biosphere (MAB) Programme. Manas (Chirang-Ripu) was also declared an Elephant Reserve in 2003. No other protected area of the country has been decorated with so many distinctions.

MANAS TIGER RESERVE

Manas Tiger Reserve encompasses an area of 2,837 sq km, within which there are 19 Reserve Forests, which also form the Park's buffer zone. These forests are spread over the districts of Kokrajhar, Bongaigaon, Barpeta, Nalbari, Kamrup and Darrang. The buffer zone forests are divided into five different territorial divisions —Kachugaon Division (819.06 sq km), Haltugaon Division (592.40 sq km), Aie Valley Division (349.48 sq km), North Kamrup Division (530.19 sq km), and Western Assam Wildlife Division (26.22 sq km). The total area thus covered is 2,317.35 sq km (this is leaving aside the 519.77 sq km of the Manas National Park, the core area of the Tiger Reserve).

MANAS NATIONAL PARK

Nestled along the Bhutan foothills, Manas National Park (which forms the core zone of the sprawling Manas Tiger Reserve) covers an area 519.77 sq km of virgin forests, with the life-giving Manas River flowing right through it. The park is divided into three ranges — Bansbari, Panbari and Bhuyapara. Considered among the best national parks in the world, Manas' uniqueness lies in its varied wildlife and breathtaking natural scenery. In addition to the big five — tiger, elephant, rhino, buffalo and gaur — as many as five species of deer inhabit the jungles of Manas.

Manas National Park

Manas RF (Part)	120 sq km
North Kamrup RF	271 sq km
Panbari RF	16.30 sq km
Kahitama RF	34.86 sq km
Kokilabari RF	77.59 sq km
TOTAL	519.77 sq km

Chronology of different status bestowed on Manas

Proposed RF	1905
Reserve Forest	1907
Game Sanctuary	1928
Wildlife Sanctuary	1950
Tiger Reserve	1973
World Heritage Site	1985
Biosphere Reserve	1989
National Park	1990
Elephant Reserve	2003

MANAS RIVER

The life-giving Manas river, to which the national park owes its name and also much of the scenic splendour, is the largest Himalayan tributary of the mighty Brahmaputra. Emerging out of the rugged mountainous terrain of Bhutan, the Manas splits into two major channels — the Beki and the Hakua — besides a number of smaller streams as it enters the plains

The two channels of Manas—the Beki and the Hakua— split at Mathanguri.

of the reserve at Mathanguri. These channels, together with other smaller rivers running through the reserve, carry enormous amounts of silt and rock from the foothills. In the process, they create alluvial terraces, comprising deep layers of deposited rock and detritus overlain with sandy loam and a thin layer of humus, so essential for the forest. The Terai tract on the south consists of fine alluvial deposits with underlying pans. Here the water table also lies

very near the surface. Flowing through the reserve, the two major rivers along with the various shifting river channels and other jungle streams provide the source of water to the animals and birds. The shifting channels also lead to the formation of swamps, particularly in the south of the park. Locally called *beels*, some of these major water bodies are Genda Beel, Dheldhela Beel, Kuri Beel, Kachomara Beel, Rabhanama Beel, etc. Besides providing shelter to a diverse range of fish and aquatic life, these beels are an important source of drinking water for animals.

FLOODS — EMERGING FURY

Floods, though occurring regularly, have not been much of a problem in Manas. This is because of its topography that gently slopes towards the south from the north. The area of the Beki basin towards the west of the park is inundated during the monsoon, but rarely for long, due to the sloping relief. Mortality of wildlife due to floods has been negligible, as animals are able to take refuge on the islands of high ground.

However, of late, the floods have been turning severe, a phenomenon that can be attributed to the widespread deforestation along the river banks on the periphery of the reserve. The direct fallout of this deforestation over the years is that the major rivers have started to shift channels frequently, and the resultant floods have been disastrous. This was evident during the floods in 2004 as the Beki changed course to flow through the Kalpani channel and washed away the bridge, snapping the park's main link with its headquarters and consequently affecting a number of fringe areas.

Although the core area of the reserve has not suffered much, particularly in terms of animal casualty, many of the fringe villages have borne the brunt of devastation by floods. In certain areas the situation is so bad that people have been residing in makeshift refugee camps for a long time.

Huge trees uprooted during the floods.

Above: Manas is home to around 600 Asiatic wild elephants.
Top: A bird of pray basking in the morning sun.

Chapter 4

WILDLIFE

Watch herds of Asiatic water buffalo ambling along the sandy bank of the Manas river or marvel at the magnificent gaurs grazing leisurely by a jungle stream. Observe in awe as elephants cross over to the other side of the river after a lengthy frolicking session in the water or gaze at a solitary rhino wallowing in the mud. Or feel your senses turn numb by the blood-curdling

roar of a tiger and you may even be thanking your stars that you have not seen it. With some luck, however, the possibility of encountering the king of the jungle, even from close quarters, is very much there.

Manas is one place where you can see the big five of the Indian jungles — the tiger (the lion is found only at Gir in Gujarat), elephant, rhino, buffalo, and gaur. The other major predator of the Indian jungles, the leopard, is also quite common in Manas.

A family of Capped langur.

Few protected areas can match Manas in its diversity of wildlife, which boasts of the highest number of protected species in India with over 40. Home to as many as 21 of the 41 Schedule I (Indian Wildlife Protection Act 1972) species of mammals, the Manas National Park is a haven for 60 species of mammals, 42 species of reptiles (11 families), over 370 bird species, seven species of amphibians (five families), 54 species of fish (19 families and nine orders), and countless different insects.

Sambar deer.

Of the 21 endangered mammal species found in Manas, some, such as the pigmy hog, the hispid hare and the golden langur are endemic to it. In fact, Manas boasts of the only viable population of the pigmy hog, the smallest and the rarest wild boar, anywhere in the world.

The avian population in Manas is as impressive as other life forms found in abundance in the park. Of the 370-odd species of birds, ten are listed in Schedule I of the Indian

A camera-trap picture of a Tiger in Manas. Courtesy: Aaranyak

Wildlife Protection Act. These flying seraphs, with their lustrous plumage and animated chirping, lend a unique touch of colour and vibrancy to the forest.

A HAVEN FOR TIGER

Among the earliest tiger reserves constituted under Project Tiger in 1973, Manas had been a tiger haven with well over a hundred of the big cat. Till the late 1980s, it harboured the highest

number of tigers in the country after the Sundarbans with a count of 123. Now, that has gone down drastically to around 40, following the decade-old social unrest in lower Assam. But 40 is still a sizeable population, considering that a national park like Ranthambhore (Rajasthan), whose claim to fame rests solely on the tiger, has a population of around 30 at its peak.

Celebrated for its power, beauty, grace and stealth, the tiger has captured the imagination of the people like no other animal. The embodiment of brute strength, savage charm and sheer elegance, the tiger is the living symbol of the Indian jungles and without question, remains the most sought-after animal in the Indian wilds. Most wildlife tourists regard their visit to a protected area incomplete without a sighting of this majestic beast. Even as the mighty tiger lords over the jungle, this magnificent but elusive creature is hard to locate unless one is well-versed in jungle lore or led by an experienced guide. Then of course, one always needs some luck to get a close look at the king of the jungle. While looking for the tiger, it always pays to keep one's ears and eyes open for any signs or sounds emanating from other animals and birds, which often give away the presence of the tiger. Different species of deer, monkeys and langurs, and birds, with their distinctive tiger alarm calls, are the best indicators of the tiger's presence nearby. Scavenger birds like vulture and magpie often betray the presence of a tiger kill, which means that the tiger is likely to be present within the vicinity, even when it may not be feeding on the carcass. Birds and monkeys, in fact, are better placed to give away the presence of a tiger, as they can effectively monitor its movements from the vantage position and safety of the trees.

ELEPHANT COUNTRY

Manas is excellent elephant country. As recently as 1988, Manas probably had the country's single largest concentration of the Asian elephant, with a population of well over a thousand. Now, after the troubled period in the late 1980s and the 1990s that did substantial harm to its fauna, the elephant population has dwindled and stands around 600, which can still be termed healthy. And the heartening thing is that of late the elephant population has recorded an upward curve. That Manas constitutes a very large protected area in the region with contiguous habitats with the forests in Bhutan in the north and the Buxa Tiger

Merging with the background—A solitary elephant browsing in the forest.

Reserve of West Bengal in the west, also explains the largely visible presence of elephants in the park. In this way, Manas forms part of a major elephant corridor, so essential for the pachyderms, who need large areas for their movement. Big herds of elephants, sometimes up to 200 members, were fairly common in Manas. Even today, these majestic animals can be frequently seen crossing the Manas river in herds.

A majestic male—Asiatic wild buffalo population of Manas is considered as the purest breed in India.

ASIATIC WATER BUFFALO

Much before it became a protected area, Manas had been an ideal habitat of the Asiatic water buffalo. While it possessed the country's highest number of this magnificent beast, the buffalo population of Manas was, and still is, regarded as the purest breed in the entire country. This is because in all other habitats of this animal, inbreeding with domestic buffalos has been a big concern. Till the late 1980s Manas

had the largest population of the buffalo with a total count of over a thousand. Over the years the buffaloes of Manas had acquired such fame that the park often came to be identified with the herds of these giant animals. The sight of these imposing beasts with the biggest span of horns grazing serenely on the bank of the Manas came to be synonymous with the park. The disturbed period took a toll on the buffaloes as well, reducing them to around 200.

Camera-trap pictures, courtesy: Aaranyak
Above: Gaur—Indian bison
Right top: Dhole—Indian wild dog and right below: A leopard.

The mammals found in Manas include the tiger, Asiatic elephant, great Indian one-horned rhinoceros, Asiatic water buffalo, gaur (Indian bison), leopard, clouded leopard, Himalayan black bear, sloth bear, golden cat, fishing cat, leopard cat, jungle cat, marbled cat, civet, binturong, pigmy hog, hispid hare, wild dog, jackal, Indian fox, hog deer, sambar, swamp deer, barking deer, spotted deer, capped langur, golden langur, Assamese macaque, otter,

Gangetic dolphin, marten, badger, weasel, pangolin, porcupine, etc.

KINGDOM AND HOME TO MAMMALS

Of the 60 mammals in Manas, 21 are Schedule I species, which is the highest in any protected area of the country. These include three primates—golden langur, capped langur and slow loris, and six from the cat family— tiger,

Slow loris.

black panther, clouded leopard, leopard cat, golden cat and fishing cat. The rest comprise sloth bear, binturong, elephant, great Indian one horned rhinoceros, Chinese pangolin, Asiatic water buffalo, swamp deer, flying squirrel, hispid hare, gangetic dolphin, wild boar and pigmy hog.

FLOCK OF FEATHERS

With over 456 species of birds recorded so far, Manas can very well stake its claim to fame

A young of Oriental pied hornbill.

on the strength of its avifauna diversity alone. Of these, ten belong to the Schedule I category. These are the black-crested baza, Lagger falcon, Shahin falcon, Bengal florican, pied hornbill, great pied hornbill, rufous-necked hornbill, wreathed hornbill, common peafowl and peacock pheasant.

Probably the avian life of the whole of Manas is yet to be properly studied. Renowned ornithologist and the present Director of the

A pair of Grey-fronted green pigeons.

Bombay Natural History Society (BNHS), Asad R Rahmani, once recorded 270 species within a small study area near Bansbari in 1990.

Among the rarest birds found in Manas is the Bengal florican. Listed in the Red Data Book of the IUCN, it is the most endangered of the 22 species of bustards in the world. Significantly, Manas perhaps has the largest known population of the Bengal florican (*Houbaropsis bengalensis*). According to Rahmani, out of a

Red jungle fowl.

world population of 400, about 80 find a secure refuge in Manas. Till the middle of the last century, the Bengal florican enjoyed an extensive habitat in the grasslands of the Himalayan foothills and the Assam Valley, with a range expanding up to Bangladesh. It is now extinct in Bangladesh and extremely rare all over its range. The few survivors are now restricted to a few pockets of grassland habitats in Manas,

A Changeable hawk eagle perched on a Simul tree.

Kaziranga, Orang, Pobitora (all in Assam), Dudhwa, Jaldapara (in Bengal), Chitwan, Sukla Phanta, Royal Bardia and Kosi Tappu (in Nepal).

Manas is among the prime habitats for most of the tall grassland species, such as the swamp francolin (*Francolinus gularis*), marsh babbler (*Turdoides longirostris*), Jerdon's babbler (*Chrysomma altirostre*), bristled grass-warbler (*Chaetornis striatus*) and many others. Manas is

A group of Red-breasted parakeets.

one of the last strongholds of the vulnerable Finn's baya (*Ploceus megarhynchus*), which is found nesting here.

As per the biome classification of BirdLife International (undated), Manas mainly lies in the Indo-Gangetic Plain (Biome 12) where 13 species are considered as biome represented. Except for the collared myna (*Acridotheres albocinctus*) which anyway, is restricted to Manipur and a small portion of adjoining Assam, all the remaining 12 species are found

A Goosander or Common merganser frolicking in Manas river.

in Manas. The presence of such a high percentage of biome-restricted species confirms that the habitat of Manas is still intact and in pristine condition.

In view of its excellent bird life and significant populations of some globally threatened species, Manas Tiger Reserve is considered one of the outstanding Important Bird Areas (IBAs) of India (BirdLife International, 2003).

A Great pied hornbill. These massive birds are extremely shy of human beings and stay in thick foliage only. This one was perched at a great distance.

A highly-endangered Manipur bush quail, last seen in 1932 in Manipur and thought to be almost extinct, was sighted at Manas National Park on June 6, 2006. Noted ornithologist Dr Anwaruddin Choudhury, who claimed to have sighted the elusive bird at the Panbari range of Manas National Park at 2.30 p.m. on June 6, termed it as an extremely important sighting, as the species had not been recorded for at least seven decades. BirdLife International puts the last authentic sighting of the Manipur bush quail in Assam even further back to 1905-07 at Mornoi in the then undivided Goalpara district of the State. This means that the bird had not been sighted for nearly a century in the State, making it among the few species that have been rediscovered after such a long gap. After the sighting of this rare species, the next logical step would be to conduct a survey of the bird, which the Forest Department plans to carry out next winter. In another important sighting the same year, Dr Choudhury spotted several white-winged wood ducks, another endangered species restricted to a few pockets in upper Assam besides a few South East Asian countries, in the park on August 3 and 4. White-winged wood ducks are a globally-threatened species found only in some South East Asian regions besides upper Assam. The Nameri National Park and the Dibru Saikhowa National Park in Assam provide a major shelter for this elusive bird, which is also the state bird of Assam.

These incidents show that the avian life of Manas National Park has not yet been exhaustively studied and recorded. It is very likely that further study will result in the addition of more species in the list of birds in Manas.

LIST OF IMPORTANT BIRDS

Critically endangered

Orient white-backed vulture *Gyps bengalensis*
Slender-billed vulture *Gyps tenuirostris*

Endangered

Greater adjutant *Leptoptilosdubious*
Bengal florican *Houbaropsis bengalensis*

Vulnerable

Spot-billed pelican *Pelecanus philippensis*
Lesser adjutant *Leptoptilos javanicus*
Greater spotted eagle *Aquila clanga*
Lesser kestrel *Falco Naumanni*
Swamp Francolin *Francolinus gularis*
Rufous-necked hornbill *Aceros nipalensis*
Hodgson's bushchat *Saxicola insignis*
Marsh babbler *Pellorneumpalustre*
Jerdon's babbler *Chrysomma altirostre*
Slender-billed babbler *Turdoides longirostris*
Black-brested parrotbill *Paradoxornis flavirostris*
Hodgson's prinia *Prinia cinereocapilla*
Bristled grass-warbler *Chaetornis striatus*
Finn's weaver *Ploceus megarhynchus*

Near threatened

Darter *Anhinga melanogaster*
Black- necked stork *Ephippiorhynchus siaticus*
Lesser grey-headed fish eagle *Ichthyophaga humilis*
Greater grey-headed fish eagle *Ichthyophaga ichthyaetus*
Cinereous vulture *Aegypius monachus*
Red-headed vulture *Sarcogyps calvus*
Great pied hornbill *Buceros bicornis*
Pallied harrier *Circus macrourus*

Endemic Bird Area 131: Assam plains

Marsh babbler *Pellorneum palustre*
Black-breasted parrotbill *Paradoxornis flavirostris*

Roaming Reptiles

Manas is home to an incredible 42 species of reptiles distributed in 11 families. Of these, 30 are snakes, nine lizards, two turtles, a tortoise and one crocodile. In a major discovery, the Assam roofed turtle (*Kachuga syhetensis*), which is among the least known, was found in Manas in 1988. It is listed under Action Plan (rating 2) by the IUCN/SSC's Tortoise and Fresh-water Turtle Specialist Group. Other rare turtles are the Eastern Hills Terrapin and the saw-backed Terrapin, about whom very little information is available. Giant pythons constitute a major part of the abundant reptile life in Manas. Specimens attaining a length of 30 feet have been recorded in the park. In May 2006, two female pythons, measuring around 30 feet and 25 feet respectively, were kept under monitoring during their incubation period after they had laid eggs.

Amphibia

So far seven amphibians distributed in five families have been recorded in Manas. These are: *Bufo melanostictus*, *Rana cyanophlyctis*, *R. limnocharis*, *R. tigrina*, *Microhyla ornata*, *Hyla sp.*, and *Cacopus globulosus*.

Fish

A total of 54 species of fish distributed under 19 families and nine orders inhabits the rivers and other water bodies in the Park. Of these, 12 are regarded as rare. These are: *Barillius shacra, B. vagra, Crossocheilus latius, Chagunius chagunio, Garra gotyla, Labeo pangusia, Puntius geluis, P. guganio, Semiplotus semiplotus, Psclorhynchus sucatio, Somileptes gongota* and *Olysa horae.*

Invertebrates

Although Manas is home to a bewildering variety of invertebrates, there has been little study on them, with the result that the information available is rather negligible. Only 103 species have been recorded so far, most of these being insects.

THE ENDANGERED ONES

Pigmy hog

The pigmy hog (*Sus salvinus*), which is the world's smallest boar, is endemic to Manas. Its size and extremely restricted habitat make it an exceptionally valuable animal from the point of conservation and scientific research. A grassland dweller, the pigmy hog normally does not exceed 65 cm in length and 25 cm in height. Its weight is about 6.5 kg. Adult males of the species are distinguished from sows by their relatively larger size, robust appearance and exposed tusks. The animal usually lives in small groups of five to ten. Its diminutive size and streamlined body enables it to attain great speed while moving through the extremely dense habitat of early successional and tall grassland. They rarely leave their grassland habitat to which they are greatly adapted. Reproduction is strongly seasonal, with well-defined birth periods that coincide with the onset of the monsoon. The litter size varies from two to six. Another distinguishing characteristic of the pigmy hog is that its nests are constructed and utilised by both the male and the female at all times of the year. It is omnivorous and feeds on roots and insects.

Golden langur

The golden langur is another highly endangered animal that is almost endemic to Manas and its adjoining areas. In India, its entire range is restricted by three rivers — the Manas in the east, the Sonkosh in the west and the Brahmaputra in the south. It finds its more secure habitat along the Indo–Bhutan border forests and inside Bhutan. Discovered by the eminent naturalist, EP Gee, in the 1950s, it was supposed to inhabit the Indo–Bhutan border only, but studies and surveys later confirmed its existence in a number of fragmented habitats within the geographical area marked by the three rivers. The golden langur is now found in at least 19 isolated pockets in the districts of Bongaigaon, Dhubri and Kokrajhar.

These fragmented habitats sheltering small populations of the golden langur are : Chirang Reserve Forest (RF)-Manas RF (in part), Ripu RF-Kochugaon RF, Manas National Park (in part)-Manas RF (in part), Chakrasila Wildlife Sanctuary, Bhairab Pahar Proposed RF, Nakkati RF, Kakiojana RF, Bamungaon RF, Abhoya rubber plantation, Nayekgaon Proposed RF, Nadanguri Hills RF, Khakarpur Proposed RF, Maelgarh Hills (Kharagaon Proposed RF), Katrigacha RF, Srigram RF, Bangalduba RF, Sarpamari RF, Bhumeswar Hills Proposed RF, Bheskamari RF. Many of these forests used to form parts of Manas Tiger Reserve in the not-so-distant past.

Rapid loss of forest cover, poaching and accidental deaths have pushed the golden langur to the brink. The Chirang RF, with an area of 593 sq km, has lost over 200 sq km during the period 1990 to 2000. It lost as much as 100 sq km during 1997-2000 alone.

Golden langurs are beautiful creatures, cream-coloured or golden-orange white, with black faces. The crown hairs are semi-erect, with a long pale beard. They live in sub-tropical moist deciduous forests and moist evergreen forests up to an altitude of 2,400 metres. Dwelling mostly in the upper canopy of the trees, they are very active during early morning and late afternoon, and prefer to rest during midday. The animals are diurnal and arboreal. Their social life is variable from one-male-multi-female troops to multi-male-multi-female troop structure. Females remain in the natal troop throughout their lives, while the males maintain troop unity and remain vigilant for predators and other groups. Females attain sexual maturity around five years of age and males around six. The birth season is July–September. Females give birth to a single offspring every two years. Soon after birth, the baby is usually handled and carried by several females.

Above: In Manas a lot of wildlife can be seen from the comfort of a jeep safa[ri]
Top: To watch the behaviour of avifauna the tourist must have a lot of pati[ence]

Chapter 5

OBSERVING WILDLIFE

To observe wildlife in Manas, or for that matter in most of the Indian jungles, it helps if the observer knows where to look for the animals. It is important from the point of view of tourism also. Because of the very nature of the Indian jungles, which are rather dense with restricted visibility, animal sighting is often rendered a tough proposition. This is more so in the case of

Rhesus macaque are as curious to look at visitors as visitors are to spot them among the foliage.

animals that do not live in herds. Unlike African safaris, which are associated with sightings of large congregations of animals, dense Indian jungles often obliterate possibilities of such large-scale viewing. The solitary and elusive nature of many of the sought-after animals, such as the tiger, also compounds the problem. In Manas also, the thick foliage and the shy nature of the animals make sighting of many species of animals somewhat difficult. But then, one can always expect to encounter a herd of Asiatic water buffaloes on the banks of the Manas, while coming across a herd of gaur, too, is another distinct possibility, although they are likely to vanish into the jungle as soon as one gets near them.

As already said, despite the immense diversity and abundance of fauna in Manas, coming across many of them is not always easy, especially for the untrained tourist. Yet, the thrill

A Hog deer spotted from the high-perch of a safari elephant. An elephant ride is a good way to spot small wild animals in the grasslands of Manas.

of exploring the jungle and the suspense of not knowing when and where a lurking animal may make an appearance, renders the task of the tourist invariably exciting.

Trekking inside Manas can be a delightful experience. In fact, it is through trekking that one can get a real 'feel' of the mystique and the grandeur of nature. Moreover, the thrill of encountering animals, or even examining animal spoors while on foot, is unlikely to be matched by any other experience. In order to get the best results out of trek, it is advisable to be accompanied by a skilled jungle tracker. Besides experienced foresters, primitive tribal groups like the Bodos, who have enjoyed a close bond with the surrounding forests for ages and are traditionally dependent on nature for their livelihood, are extremely knowledgeable about jungle crafts and hence make excellent trackers. Many such tribesmen possess amazing understanding and information about the jungles and their inhabitants, and are experts in reading tracks and trails and other signs, which otherwise might mean nothing to the uninitiated eyes and ears of the ordinary tourist.

Taking a boat ride can be another rewarding experience as far as viewing of wildlife is concerned. One can get into a boat at Mathanguri and then float downstream up to Bansbari. It is most likely that one would encounter animals on the riverbanks during the boat ride. EP Gee, the renowned naturalist, has described it one of the best ways to observe wildlife in Manas.

Above: Bodo women on the periphery of Manas National Park near Kokilabari.

Top: Mustard fields near Bansbari.

Chapter 6

THE PEOPLE OF MANAS

Beautiful damsels sway gracefully to the beat of the dhol (drum) and the siphung (flute), as the campfire lights up the atmosphere in bright yellow. It is the Bagromba dance of the Bodo tribe, celebrating the harvesting of crops. Bodos, a major tribe of Assam, are also the dominant inhabitants in the villages near Manas. Among the earliest inhabitants of Assam, the Bodos are

endowed with a culture as vibrant as the jungles of Manas. Any traveller visiting Manas must make it a point not to miss out on the rich culture and heritage of the Bodos. For the anthropologically inclined too, the tribal villages near Manas can provide enough material for study and research. A tribe renowned for its courage and conviction, the Bodos have enjoyed a traditional association with the forests since the earliest times.

Fatemabad Tea Estate on the edge of Manas National Park at Bansbari.

The Assamese, the Bengalis, the Nepalis and the tea-tribes account for the rest of the population living around the Manas National Park — all boasting of their own unique culture and traditions. The tea-tribe population is mainly confined to the Fatemabad Tea Estate, situated on the fringe of the Bansbari Range. The tea garden adds to the attraction of Manas, especially for the foreign tourist. For those who want to have a first-hand account of how tea is

A glorious sunrise on a misty morning at the tea estate near Bansbari.

Life at the tea gardens—an added tourist attraction at Bansbari.

grown and produced, a visit to the tea estate, said to be the second largest in Asia, is a must.

Manas offers tourists a chance to experience first-hand the idyllic country life of Assam. By spending some time in the nearby tribal villages, one can get a lot of insight into the traditions, customs, culture and lifestyle of the people.

For those interested in folk culture, traditional dances of different tribes are arranged in the resort near the Bansbari Range, where one

Bansbari Lodge run by Assam Bengal Navigation Company, provides an excellent base to explore Manas National Park. Nature guide services, jeep and elephant safaris can all be organised from the comfort of this resort overlooking the tea gardens.

can enjoy the lively presentation of different ethnic cultures, sitting in the comforts of a bonfire. There the tourist has also the option to choose from among a number of mouth-watering indigenous cuisines.

As you travel along the narrow, winding village roads before entering Manas, you will be struck by the simple, quiet and unhurried country life of Assam. You will be savouring every bit of the idyllic countryside—vast

expanses of ready-to-harvest paddy that paint the landscape in gold, cows and goats grazing leisurely in the fields, a lone cowherd—with a flute to his mouth—taking his animals back home against the backdrop of the setting sun, and thatched houses on either side of the road with vegetable gardens in the compounds—all

of which is sure to remain etched in your memory forever.

Closer to Manas, most of the human habitations near the Park occur along its southern boundary. There are some 60 revenue villages, besides one forest village that is inside the Park, situated within a distance of 2 km from

The drive from Barpeta Road to Bansbari, though a bumpy ride, offers some beautiful views of river, that at some places, flows next to the road.

the Park boundary. The total population would be more than 53,000, with over 80 per cent falling in Barpeta district, and the rest in Bangaigaon.

There is no town or industry in the immediate proximity of the Manas National Park. Away from the mainstream life of cities and towns, these fringe villages have not seen much development since the country's independence. This is adequately reflected in their access to education, health care and employment avenues, which is rather poor. The infrastructure, too, is extremely inadequate. Roads, which remain dusty and bumpy during the winter, turn muddy during the monsoon days.

As per a survey conducted in 1997, the literacy rate in these villages varied from 33.9 per cent to 11.9 per cent. Most of the villagers are poor, landless labourers or marginal farmers.

Bodo women are known for their weaving skills.

The absence of an agro-economic infrastructure and irrigational facilities, coupled with the lack of modern farm techniques has ensured that productivity remains low. A major part of the income, ranging between 60 per cent to 80.9 per cent of the total household earnings, is found to originate from the main occupation, which is variable. The second important source of income is divided equally between crop production and forest resources.

PEOPLE'S PARTICIPATION : THE KOKILABARI INITIATIVE

While the relationship between the fringe villagers and the Forest Department is not exactly healthy in most parts of Manas, marked as it is by constant friction between the two, the Kokilabari area under the Bhuyanpara Range has shown that it is not difficult to work hand in hand, when conservation becomes the common objective. The concept of people's participation in the conservation process, though still at a nascent stage in Manas, has definitely made a headstart at Kokilabari, thanks to the initiative of an enterprising NGO (Maozigendri Eastern Manas Eco-Tourism Society), the local Chapaguri-Kokilabari unit of the All Bodo Students' Union (ABSU) and some innovative thinking on the part of the Park authorities.

The impact made by the combined effort of the three is visible on many fronts. Poaching and tree-felling in and around Kokilabari has come down to a trickle, a number of poachers have surrendered, the soured relationship between the department and the fringe villagers has softened

ABSU office at Kokilabari—All Bodo Students' Union has done some remarkable thinking on the eco-management and protection in the eastern part of Manas National Park.

a lot, and most significantly, there is now a growing awareness about the need to protect, preserve and promote Manas.

The transformation at Kokilabari is nothing short of amazing, considering the fact that it was among the most vulnerable and disturbed areas in Manas, where killing of animals and tree-felling were rampant till very recently. The last rhino of Manas was killed in Kokilabari three years back (although unconfirmed reports

Fearless foot soldiers of Manas Maozigendri Ecotourism Society patrol the eastern parts of the national park.

attribute one or two rhinos still in Manas). It used to be a major hub of trade in animal body parts as well. The notoriety of poachers from Kokilabari was such that they were 'hired' to hunt even in faraway forests like the Kaziranga National Park.

Joyshran Basumatary, a hardcore poacher who poached for nearly 35 years in Manas, seems a changed man now, after he was persuaded to surrender by the NGO a couple of

Rolls reversed—Yesterday's poachers are guardians of the wild today.

years back. Currently working as a labourer in a road rebuilt by the NGO, he says: 'I killed a lot of rhinos, elephants and deer but gave up poaching as I realised the immorality of the trade. Although my earning today is less than what I earned as a poacher, there is more peace now as the constant fear of being hounded by the law-enforcers is not there'.

A TALE OF TWO POACHERS

Joyshran Basumatary used to know Manas like his own backyard, as he roamed in the jungles, killing animals at will. This continued for over thirty-five years during which he took the lives of numerous animals, mostly deer, rhino, elephant, buffalo and tiger. His 'name and fame' spread far and wide, and his 'expertise' became a much sought-after thing among the wildlife traders. His 'services' were hired for utilisation in other protected areas as well,

Locally made muzzle loading guns, confiscated from unlawful elements, now provide fire power to guard against activities of few remaining poachers and smugglers.

including Kaziranga. But it seems a change of heart is never impossible. Joyshran renounced his life of the slaughterer, and turned over a new leaf. A changed man, now he is devoting himself in engagements that contribute to the well-being of the park.

While poaching continues to be a persisting headache for the park authorities, there are instances galore when poachers like Joyshran gave up their nefarious activities and not only joined the mainstream but actually became partners in the conservation process. With their vast knowledge about the forest, poachers, once they give up hunting, can become assets to the Forest Department. They can also be of great use as informers and in checking forest crimes.

Buddhiswar Bodo (32) is another hardcore poacher who, like Joyshran, preferred to join the mainstream after a pretty long stint as a hunter. Buddhiswar, whose eight-year killing spree in Manas prior to his surrender a couple of years back, accounted for the lives of a number of rhinos and 'countless deer and elephants', says, 'I was a habitual hunter, and often we used to go out in groups of 30–40 to hunt'. Buddhiswar's hunting career, ironically, was cut short after he was badly mauled by an injured wild boar. However, he insists that he had already made up his mind to surrender when the accident took place. 'I was really very repentent about the killings I had made, and would have surrendered anyway before the boar injured me.' Now Buddhiswar seems quite happy and contented doing odd jobs for the Forest Department.

Above: Grasslands of Manas National Park—An ideal rhino habitat.
Top: An image from the past.

Chapter 7

THE RHINOLAND THAT WAS

While the Manas National Park used to be an important rhinoland, harbouring over a hundred of the species till the late 1980s, the prolonged social unrest throughout the 1990s took a heavy toll on many animals. The great Indian one-horned rhinoceros was the greatest casualty, as almost the entire population was wiped out. Although the last rhino in the Park was said to

have been killed near Kokilabari in 2002, the good news is that one or two animals were able to escape the slaughter and are still surviving in the park. The writer himself witnessed a juvenile rhino near Goruchora in November 2004, while another full-grown adult was also reported near Kokilabari about the same time. This is extremely encouraging news for the Forest authorities, conservationists, and the general people alike.

Following the near-extinction of the great Indian one-horned rhinoceros in Manas, Forest authorities and wildlife experts are now working out a strategy to reintroduce a viable rhino population in the park. As the first step towards the translocation experiment, a three-year-old female rhino from the Animal Rescue Centre at the Kaziranga National Park was released in Manas in February 2006.

This rhino, now confined to a one square-km area surrounded by an electrified fence, is under constant monitoring of armed forest personnel. Christened *Mainao*, the rhino seems to have adapted to the new surroundings, as it spends time grazing and relaxing. It drinks natural water available inside the enclosed area and has also started depositing dung, which the Forest officials have described as positive signs. At times, it was also seen displaying traits associated with wild rhinos, despite the fact that it was hand-reared at Kaziranga's wildlife rescue centre right from infancy.

'The first signs are good, and it has showed no stress,' Field Director Rabha says. Apart from Forest Department personnel, experts from

Wildlife Trust of India (WTI) were also providing necessary support in the exercise.

The real challenge, however, will begin when the time comes to release it in the wild. It is a long process, and will take at least a year.

If the venture turns out to be successful, 25–30 rhinos from Kaziranga and the Pobitora Wildlife Sanctuary would be introduced in Manas in a phased manner. All this would be under the Forest Department's ambitious rhino translocation plan, which aims at having a sustainable rhino population spread across seven protected areas of the State. As of now, the entire rhino population of the State (2,006 numbers in the 2006 census) is confined to just three protected areas—the Kaziranga National Park, the Pobitora Wildlife Sanctuary and the Orang National Park. Under the Rhino Vision 2020, under implementation by the Forest Department with support from the WWF and International Rhino Foundation, rhinos are to be reintroduced in the Manas National Park, the Dibru-Saikhowa National Park, the Laokhowa Wildlife Sanctuary and the Burhachapori Wildlife Sanctuary. The Orang National Park would also get some rhinos, as its rhino population has dwindled considerably over the past one decade. The main objective of Rhino Vision 2020 is to attain a 3,000-strong rhino population spread across these seven protected areas by the year 2020.

Above: The forest bungalow at Mathanguri.
Top: A view of the river between Barpeta Road and Bansbari.

Chapter 8

TOURISM

The road was bumpy and we all felt it even as the skillful driver tried his best to negotiate the potholes on the narrow road smoothly. As the main road to Manas from Barpeta Road (a distance of just 22 km) had been closed for quite some time following the breach of a bridge over the Kalpani, we had to take a big detour while passing through another route. The jerky road

ensured that we could not move at a decent speed, making the journey much longer and arduous.

We had set out from the Field Director's Office at Barpeta Road at 9 a.m. and finally, after driving for around three hours, reached our destination, the Bansbari Range Office. There we rested for a while, and the warm hospitality accorded to us by the Ranger, Mohan Chandra Brahma, was enough to make us forget the effects of the tiresome journey. Brahma, a cheerful and energetic person, sounded rather apologetic about the poor road conditions. From Bansbari we left for Mathanguri, the most scenic place in the Manas National Park, situated on the banks of the roaring Manas River. Brahma also accompanied us this time. Bansbari to Mathanguri is a short journey lasting around half an hour. In stark contrast, however, was this drive compared to our earlier journey up to

Peacocks—A rewarding sight seen very often between Bansbari and Mathanguri.

Bansbari. With dense forests on either side of the gravelled, even road, it seemed that the mysterious Manas was slowly opening up to enfold us in her soothing embrace. Then, all of a sudden, the jungle calm was shattered by a trumpeting elephant, which appeared right in front of us. It was obvious that the animal was more surprised than us, as it dashed off into the woods immediately. We also came across a huge gaur very near the roadside. The majestic animal, which stood over six feet tall and must have weighed a tonne, transfixed its gaze on us and watched us as we slowly went past it. Peacocks we encountered several times during our brief journey. Among other wildlife we noticed were capped langurs and a number of deer. Manas boasts of as many as five varieties of deer.

It was almost dusk when we stopped at Mathanguri, where we were to spend the night. We were struck by the landscape of the place, which was simply out of this world. The view before us was such that words are inadequate to describe the grandeur. The truth is that one could only feel it and not describe it. We realised immediately what makes people visit Manas again and again—so captivating is its charm.

A visit to Manas is always an unforgettable experience. The vibrant wilderness of Manas, coupled with its unparalleled scenic grandeur, provides a unique opportunity for not just the adventure-seeker and nature-lover, but for anyone who wants to take a break from the daily humdrum of city life and relax under the soothing touch of Mother Nature. It is said that the air of Manas is endowed with a unique freshness and healing attributes due to the presence of a number of medicinal plants— something the visitor invariably feels as he or she enters Manas. This certainly makes the stay in Manas an invigorating experience.

The picturesque Manas National Park had always been a favourite destination with both domestic and foreign tourists, before it was hit by a prolonged social disturbance in the late 1980s and 1990s. But things have turned normal now, and the Park has again started witnessing a reasonable flow of tourists for the last few seasons. Manas is the place where pristine forests, breathtaking landscape and diverse wildlife combine to lend it a unique charm, a rare sight anywhere in the world. The panoramic view at Mathanguri, where the meandering Manas surges out of the rugged hills

A picturesque drive through the woodlands of Manas.

of Bhutan and splits into two channels, is a sight to behold. A visit to Manas is truly a balm for sore eyes and stressed souls.

Recently, an initiative aimed at developing community tourism was taken up jointly by the Chapaguri–Kokilabari unit of the All Bodo Students' Union (ABSU), the Maozigendri Eastern Manas Eco-Tourism Society, the Siliguri-based Help Tourism and Ashoka Holidays. A special tour package, Manas-100, that includes elephant ride, jeep safari, trekking and tracking, bird-watching from Hornbill Point and a Bengal florican survey, has also been launched. The fringe villages are expected to get an adequate share of the activities in the form of offering traditional home stays in cottages, functions showcasing traditional folk culture and lifestyle, introduction to traditional weaving practices and methods of distilling country liquor, etc.

As of now there is just one forest bungalow at Mathanguri besides one tourist lodge constructed by the Assam Tourism Development Corporation (ATDC) at Bansbari, which has been leased out to a private operator, Assam Bengal Navigation Company. It basically caters to foreign tourists, making Manas a part of a state-wide packaged tour through a number of important tourist spots of Assam like Tezpur, Kaziranga, Majuli, etc.

Keeping in mind the rush of tourists to Manas, the authorities would do well to restore the few accommodations at Mathanguri that have all but crumbled due to years of non-use and neglect.

If tourism gets the much-needed thrust from

the authorities, it will definitely hasten the healing process of this premier national park of the country.

Wildlife viewing apart, Manas offers ample scope for other excitements for the adventure-seeker. White water rafting on the frothing Manas River is one attractive proposition for the adventure tourist. Trekking is another much-preferred pastime, and one can tread the path amidst the 'lovely, dark and deep' woods up to the undulating, green hills of Bhutan.

Another attraction unique to Manas is the Mahout Training Centre, which is the first of its kind in Asia, imparting training in various aspects of elephant rearing and training. Training of elephants after they are captured in the wild has been an enduring tradition in Assam. Since time immemorial the practice of catching and training elephants has evolved into an art, and history and legend alike are replete with references to the glorious time-tested tradition of the State. The epic, *Mahabharata*, describes how Bhagadutta, the great king of Pragjyotishpur (present-day Assam) fought valiantly for the Kauravas in the Kurukshetra war with his hundreds of elephants.

The Mahout Training Centre, set up in 2004 at the Bansbari Range, is expected to contribute a lot towards preserving and updating the wealth of traditional knowledge of elephant management that exists in the State and the North-east. The two classical methods of elephant-capturing, the Mela Shikar and the Kheda Shikar, originated and evolved in the North-east before those were adopted in other

States. This vast knowledge base had hitherto remained untapped due to the absence of any effort to organise the mahouts and the *phandis* (elephant-catchers) who are an illiterate, disorganised and scattered lot. This is in sharp contrast to the present situation where management of elephants has become a specialised job requiring continuous upgradation of their knowledge and skills. In spite of the restrictions imposed on tree-felling and elephant-capturing, domesticated elephants still can be put to diverse uses like jungle patrolling, anti-depredation drives, animal census operations, tourism purposes, etc.

The Mahout Training Centre at Bansbari deals with various aspects of elephant management, right from capturing in the wild to caring and training. Elephants and humans have enjoyed a traditional bonding in Assam throughout the ages — something adequately reflected in the innumerable folksongs and other literature that glorify the elephant. Way back in the 18th century, when the State was ruled by the mighty Ahoms, an all-comprehensive treatise on various aspects of elephant rearing, training and management, *Hastibidyarnava,* was composed by the great scholar, Sukumar Borkayat.

Above: Manas—a storehouse of biodiversity.
Top: A view of the wooded Bhutan hills.

Chapter 9

MANAS BIOSPHERE RESERVE

Manas Tiger Reserve was recognised as a Biosphere Reserve on March 14, 1989, making it the first biosphere reserve of Assam. Till date, Dibru-Saikhowa in the upper Assam districts of Dibrugarh and Tinsukia is the only other Biosphere Reserve of the State. Spread over a sprawling area of 2,837 sq km from the Sonkosh river in the west and the Dhansiri river in the

A stream near Daimari in the eastern part of Manas National Park.

east (the core area of 519.77 sq km forms the Manas National Park), Manas represents best the tropical humid Bengal rain forests in the Indo–Malayan realm. The entire reserve is spread over a belt of forests lying along the Himalayan forest hills to the north of the Brahmaputra Valley, in a linear belt about 50 km wide at the broadest position in the west and gradually narrowing towards the east. The northern boundary forms part of the common international border with Bhutan, and the mixed forest belt is contiguous with that of the Bhutan hills (called the Royal Manas National Park). All the southern boundaries verge on the cultivation areas and village settlements.

Located between 26.30 degree to 27.0 degree north latitudes and between 91.5 degree to 90.0 degree east longitudes covering the six districts of Barpeta, Nalbari, Kamrup, Bongaigaon, Kokrajhar and Darrang, the average elevation of the area is 85 metres above mean sea level.

When we look into the primary criteria of Biosphere Reserves, the immensely rich biodiversity of Manas comes to the fore. These criteria are:

(a) The area should be representative of the overall biota of the region.

(b) It should represent the pristine natural ecosystem.

(c) Biological diversity, both in terms of plant and animal species in all its forms, is to be preserved.

(d) The area selected should be such that these could be conserved in its naturalness and biological diversity with least anthropogenic pressure and other disturbances.

The secondary criteria are:

(a) The area having rare and endangered species, both plant and animal, should get priority for setting up of the Biosphere Reserve.

(b) There should be diversity of soil and climatic conditions and all indigenous varieties of plants and animals.

(c) The area should have potential for preservation of traditional tribal or rural modes of living for harmonious use of the environment.

It was on the basis of the above criteria that the Indian National (Man and Biosphere) Committee identified 14 sites including Manas in 1979 as potential Biosphere Reserves, covering as many as nine of the twelve bio-geographic regions within India.

A Biosphere Reserve entails one or more core zones, which are securely protected sites of biological diversity and minimally disturbed ecosystem. Then there should be a well-defined buffer zone or zones, which usually surround or adjoin the core zone and are used for cooperative activities involving the local communities that is compatible with sound ecological practices. A flexible transitional area or area of cooperation is another element. This may contain a variety of agricultural activities, settlements and other uses, and in which local communities, management agencies and other stakeholders work together to manage and develop the area's resources in a manner that is sustainable.

Garden of nature—A view on way to Mathanguri from Bansbari.

The 2,837-sq km Manas Tiger Reserve (also the Biosphere Reserve), the core area of which forms the Manas National Park, is spread over the districts of Barpeta, Kokrajhar, Bongaigaon, Kamrup, Darrang and Nalbari. While the core area is without human habitation except for one forest village called Agrong, the buffer zone is interspersed with a number of forest villages, inhabited mostly by the Bodo tribe, Nepali graziers, and Assamese and Bengali agriculturists. The southern boundary runs along agricultural fields, and also has a tea estate in its periphery. Only the northern boundary that runs parallel to the Bhutan hills is virtually undisturbed. The declaration of the forests on the Bhutan side as a national park by the Bhutan authorities has ensured that a vast tract of nearly 3,300 sq km of contiguous forests is protected in both the countries. The Manas river, flowing southwards from Bhutan to India after

Manas is full of exotic plant life.

descending from the Himalayas, marks the boundary of the forests near Mathanguri.

The altitude of Manas National Park varies from 50 metres to 200 metres. The terrain is mostly flat, with a gentle but marked slope towards the south. A number of rivers crisscross the Park from north to south. The Manas river originates in the Himalayas in Bhutan and after bisecting the Park into two parts, joins the mighty Brahmaputra some 50 km south of the Manas Tiger Reserve.

CLIMATE

The climate of Manas is moist tropical, and the annual rainfall is around 4,000 mm. It receives most of the rainfall between June and September, although the rains generally start in March and continue up to as late as October. Summer in Manas can be sweltering, with the maximum temperature shooting up to 36 degree Celsius, while the winters can be equally freezing, with temperatures plummeting to 5 degree Celsius.

VEGETATION

Over 700 species of plants (Pteridophytes and Angiosperms) have been recorded so far in Manas. As not much research has gone into its plant life, it is very likely that many species have gone unrecorded. Most of the plants are dicotylendons and monocotylendons.

The forests of Manas National Park are classified into six types, in accordance with the classification system of Champion and Seth.

(a) Sub-Himalayan high alluvial semi-evergreen forests: This formation occurs mostly along the northern belt of Manas. There is an emergent layer of Bhelu (*Tetrameles nudiflora*), which is the characteristic of this type. Below this emergent layer of deciduous species, the top storey is formed by Hatipolia (*Pterospermum acerifolium*), Bogijan (*Eugenia praecox*), Banderdima (*Dysoxilum binectariferum*), Bonsum (*Phoebe goalparensis*), Amari (*Amoora wallichii*), Parali (*Stereospermum personatum*), Bogipoma (*Chukrassia velutina*), Khokon (*Duabanga grandiflora*), etc. The middle storey is made up of Banderdima, Jia (*Linnea coromandelica*), Udal, Hatipolia, Sopa (*Michelia sp.*), etc. The ground cover consists of evergreen shrubs like *Morinda angustifolia*, Alpina zingber, Desmodium, Fern, etc. Canes are very occasional in occurrence.

(b) Eastern Bhabar type forests: Pure patches of Koroi (*Albizzia procera*) occur in the

Above and right: A large variety of fungus can be found on the forest floor of Manas.

moist parts along the banks of the streams and rivers in Manas. Koroi predominates such patches, and the occasional associates are Simul, Jam, Bhelker (*Trewia polycarpa*), Gamari (*Gmelina arborea*), and Udal. Young Bhelker, *Macuranga* sp. and occasional Palas account for the middle storey. The ground cover is made up of ferns, *colocassia* sp., *Solanum* sp., etc. with occasional *Ziziphus* sp. and *Eupatorium odoratum* in open locations. Infestation of the climber *Mikenia* sp. is rather heavy, and forms a thick cover on the ground.

(c) East Himalayan moist mixed deciduous forest: This type of forest occupies some of the hill slopes near the northern boundary and the terraces or plateau in the Bhabar areas. It also occurs as stripes and belts along water courses in the moist of the savannah formations. The forest appears to be transitional in nature and is likely to pass on to the next stage (semi-

evergreen) in the presence of favourable circumstances. The top-storey species are *Premma* sp, Siris, Pahari, *Bauhnia* sp, Hatipolia, *Morus* sp., etc. The middle storey is predominated by saplings of Sida, (*Lagerstromia parviflora*), Bohera, Hilika (*Terminalia chebula*), Bhelkar, Jam, Jamuk, Sonaru, etc. The undergrowth and the ground cover varies according to the canopy conditions and moisture regime of the soil. In moist locations, ferns, Agexotum, *Alpina* sp. occur as ground cover. In open locations, *Eupatorium odoratum*, *Imperata cylindrical*, *Flemingia* sp., *Leea* sp., etc. occur as ground cover. Among climbers, *Mikenia* sp. predominates in all areas not covered by a close canopy.

(d) Assam Valley semi-evergreen Forests: Existent in patches in the moist soils of the Terai belt in the Manas Reserve Forest and the Panbari Reserve Forest of the Park, the top storey species

Nature's recycling at work—This elephant dung will soon be converted into rich manure by these fast-growing mushrooms.

in this formation are Parali, Hatipolia, Owtenga, Poma Urium, Jamuk, Bahera, etc. Gahora, Maskoita, Kuhir, Morolia, Kathiakoroi, etc. account for the middle storey. The ground cover is made up of <u>*Leea*</u> sp., *Desmoduim* sp., *Alpinis* sp., *Melastoma* sp., and various monocotyledonous plants.

(e) Eastern wet alluvial grassland (Terai formation): In badly drained and low-lying locations, there is a change in the composition and in such locations occasional Koroi, Urium, Owtenga and Bhelkor and Simul come up. *Saccharum procerum*, *S. spontaneum*, *Apluda aristata*, *Phragmites*, *Erianthus* sp., etc. are the grass found in this type. The extreme form of this type in locations having perennial water (swamps), is devoid of trees, and the vegetation consists of *Eicchoria* sp., *Nyuprioides* sp., *Vessia*, *Polygonum* sp., *Phragmites*, etc.

In general, both Terai and Savannah grassland occupy nearly 40 per cent of the total park area. Two theories are in vogue regarding the nature of these grasslands.

According to one theory, Savannah and Terai are edaphic climaxes caused by soil conditions. Terai type occurs in areas with high water table and successive layers of debris, humus, sand, silt and clay. Savannah type occurs in the Bhabar areas with a low water table and dry sandy and loamy soil formation with a humus layer. The second theory, on the other hand, attributed the grasslands as a whole to a stage of arrested succession, i.e. biotic climax originating from the regular practice of burning of grasslands.

The lower plant species still remains an unstudied and unexplored lot. The Park provides an excellent habitat for conservation of flora, where very interesting and rare plants such as *Reinwardtia indica, Esmodium motorium, Pueravia subspicata, Bidens pilosa, Chiloschista lunifera, Oplismenus megaphyllus, Mangifera sylvatica,* etc. occur.

Grasslands—A vital part of Manas habitat.

GRASSLAND MANAGEMENT

While grasslands constituted almost half of Manas National Park's total area of 519.77 sq km area till some years back, recent satellite imagery and ground verification have confirmed that there has been a marked decline of ten to twelve per cent in the grassland cover, thereby

reducing it to around 38 per cent of the Park area.

The invasion of *Leea asiatica* (Aathubhanga Ban) and *Bombax ceiba* (Simalu) is mainly responsible for the shrinking of grassland habitat in Manas. The invasion, again, has its roots in anthropogenic factors like resource exploitation, grazing pressure, man-made fire, etc.

Grasslands constitute a very important part of the Park, much of which is tall with rich

Controlled patch-wise burning is an effective grassland management practice that checks the march of woodlands into grasslands. Young trees of invasive species like Bombax ceiba *can't withstand fire and half-burnt stems are happily consumed by elephants.*

diversity. Besides pigmy hog and hispid hare, which are the two most endangered grassland dwellers, tiger, elephant, rhino, buffalo, hog deer, otter, Bengal florican, various partridges, peacock, etc. are also greatly dependent on the grassland habitat. Moreover, grasslands act as corridors for movement of many animals.

This loss of grassland cover, though not yet at an alarming level, is certainly a disturbing development that has the potential to cause a

lot of harm in the future unless treated in a scientific manner at the earliest.

Phyto-invasion by some undershrubs and tree species has quickened the shrinking and degrading of grassland in the Park. Significantly, such invasion is fast in the disturbed areas. The invasion of *Bombax ceiba* is a particularly disquieting phenomenon, as the species is fire-resistant. Early burning (late October to November, mid-December) is an effective tool for dealing with this invasive species because the seed-dispersal period of Simalu can be evaded through this.

Late burning is for a specific purpose, for which special care and monitoring is needed. Periodic burning has been the major method for grassland management in Manas. The normal procedure followed is to map the grassland area and demarcate the potential pigmy hog and Bengal florican habitat by cutting wide fire lines to form blocks of no less than two hectares.

Fresh grass shoots appear in the ash-enriched soil soon after burning of tall dry grass. This is welcome by small herbivores like deer.

Simalu saplings are to be hacked before they are four years old.

Grazing of cattle has been a persistent irritant in grassland management, as it can lead to a lot of undesirable invasion from weeds. 'Supervision of mosaic burning when extended all over the grassland blocks, is difficult due to absence of beats,' says Field Director Rabha.

Research into the grassland ecosystem vis-à-vis the pigmy hog is on. 'Pigmy hog and Bengal florican habitat can be easily restored just by stopping anthropogenic fire, domestic grazing and minimising the resource collection. In fact, the area can restored within a year,' says Pranjal Bezbarua, a field botanist.

Floods are a natural tool for creating grasslands. Floods create small sand bars that have the potential to become grassland areas in the near future.

Plant life is exceptionally rich and diverse in Manas, with over 700 plant species, including new records, having been collected from the Biosphere Reserve. It may go up to 1,000 if the buffer areas, especially the Indo–Bhutan border, are properly explored.

The Park has very good patches of evergreen, semi-evergreen, and mixed deciduous forests with very rich diversity. A typical feature of the Manas vegetation has been its amazing self-sustaining and regenerating capacity.

Most plants in Manas have great medicinal and economic value, and are effectively used by the people living in fringe areas. Of late, smuggling of medicinal plants on the western buffer has emerged as a disturbing trend.

Above: Royal Manas National Park of Bhutan—just across the river at Mathanguri.

Top: Golden langur—star attraction of Royal Manas National Park.

Chapter 10

ROYAL MANAS NATIONAL PARK

Royal Manas National Park in Bhutan, which, towards its south, forms a contiguous belt of very rich forests with the Manas National Park in Assam, is the largest and the most representative of the tropical and sub-tropical ecosystems in the Himalayan kingdom. It is also connected to the Black Mountains National Park on the north. Teeming with thousands of

species of flora and fauna, many of which are globally endangered, the Royal Manas National Park boasts of being not just the most diverse protected area in Bhutan but also one of the global biodiversity hotspots.

Nestled in the hilly terrain of south-central Bhutan, it was declared a wildlife sanctuary in 1966 by the Royal Government of Bhutan after it had been preserved as a reserve forest for a long time. The declaration also made Royal Manas the first protected area of the country.

After over two decades, it was elevated to a national park in 1993. Now it forms the crown jewel of an extensive protected area system that covers more than 26 per cent of Bhutan's land.

Much of Bhutan's forests range between the tropical and the temperate, and Royal Manas

Above: A view of Bhutan hills.

Far above: A rare camera-trap picture of a tiger in the Bhutan hills. Photo courtesy: WWF Bhutan.

happens to be the only area containing in itself the mosaic of this wide range of habitats. An astonishing 92 per cent of its 1,023 sq km is under forest vegetation, including vast areas of tropical monsoon forests interspersed with swaths of savannah grasslands and wide riverbeds.

Rugged, mountainous terrain with moderately steep slopes mark much of Royal Manas. Climatic conditions of the park vary a great deal in terms of rainfall and temperature. On a broad scale, variability in rainfall can be attributed to the May–September monsoon, with records of rainfall up to 1,200 mm. Thunderstorms are common during summer, and the rivers assume the forms of terrifying torrents. Rainfall, however, is negligible during the winter, when temperatures may drop by almost 10 degree Centigrade.

Animal life in Royal Manas is extremely rich and diverse. It is highly representative of the

Royal Manas National Park is also famous for a very large number of wild flowers.

Indo–Malayan species, including the endangered tiger, Asian elephant, one-horned rhinoceros, clouded leopard, Himalayan black bear, pangolin and Gangetic dolphin. Among the most important animals finding a safe refuge in Royal Manas is the highly-endangered golden langur. Found nowhere else except in the Manas National Park and a few fragmented and degraded habitats in lower Assam, the golden langur probably has its last shelter in Royal Manas. Some other rare species endemic to the Eastern Himalayan foothills, the pigmy hog and the hispid hare, are also major inhabitants of Royal Manas.

The bird life of Royal Manas compares favourably with the best found anywhere in the world, with over 365 species having been officially recorded so far. Add to this another 200 believed to be in residence, the avifauna of Royal Manas is truly outstanding. Some globally-

A specimen of exotic flora from Royal Manas National Park.

threatened species such as the rufous-necked hornbill, Pallas' fishing eagle, great white-bellied heron, spotted wren-babbler, blue-headed rock thrush and emerald cuckoo occur here in fairly substantial numbers.

Equally varied and amazing is the plant life of this Himalayan protected area. Over 900 plant species identified so far, many are of immense commercial, medicinal, traditional and religious significance. These include many species of bamboo, rhododendrons and orchids; Ficus trees, the dominant canopy that provides food for numerous animals, birds and insects; *Rauvolfia setrpentina*, a very rare medicinal shrub, and *Aesandra butyracea*, a valuable fruit and oil-seed tree.

The flora and fauna of Royal Manas still remains unstudied. Only partial lists are available for the Park's reptiles, amphibians and fish. It is important that thorough studies are done so that a better understanding of the ecosystem is generated for effective management.

APPENDICES

MANAS FACT FILE

GETTING THERE

AIR: The Lokapriya Gopinath Bordoloi (LGB) International Airport at Borjhar, Guwahati, is the nearest airport. It has direct/connecting flights with Kolkata, Delhi and Mumbai besides Bangkok. It is 130 km from Barpeta Road (Manas National Park and Tiger Reserve headquarters), 150 km from Bansbari, 170 km from Mathanguri, and 140 km from Kokilabari. Taxis, buses and mini buses are available from or near the airport.

RAIL: Barpeta Road is the nearest railhead (just one km from the Park headquarters and 120 km from Guwahati, the State capital). Taxis are available from the station to Manas.

ROAD: Barpeta Road, a bustling commercial centre, is well-connected with the rest of the State through the National Highway-31. It is 120 km from Guwahati, and there are daily buses to and from Guwahati. The distance from the Park headquarters at Barpeta Road to Bansbari (where the Park starts) is 20 km, and another 20 km through the jungle to Mathanguri, the most scenic spot of Manas.

Barpeta Road also enjoys good connectivity with Barpeta-Hajo-Guwahati, Bongaigaon-Siliguri (West Bengal). Buses and taxis are available in most of these towns.

ACCOMMODATION

Accommodation inside Manas is limited, making it even more exotic to visit. There is an inspection bungalow of the Forest Department at Mathanguri with five double-bed rooms with attached toilets. One, however, has to bring one's own supplies, especially ration, for the stay, which can be cooked by the forest staff. The trouble is worth taking, for Mathanguri is easily the most picturesque location to stay. For bookings, one should contact the Field Director or the Deputy Field Director of Manas (Phone- 0366-261413, 260289).

The Bansbari Lodge (tariff: INR 1000 plus taxes) at the entrance of the Park and only a few metres from the elephant riding point is another comfortable lodge run by an Indo–British joint venture company, Assam Bengal Navigation with offices in Guwahati and London. It has 16 simple but comfortable rooms with twin beds and attached bathrooms that have running hot and cold water facility. There is an in-house power generator for continuous electricity supply. *The Independent* newspaper of the UK had adjudged the Bansbari lodge as one of the five best jungle retreats of India in March 2006. The cuisine includes Indian, Continental and Chinese and meals are provided at an extra cost (INR 500 plus taxes for three meals). The lodge organises elephant and jeep safaris, a dance performance for groups in the evening around a camp fire, boat rides, village visits and nature walks with resident naturalists. With prior notice, the lodge can arrange transfers to and from Guwahati at an extra cost. It also offers as a Jungle Plan on both twin-share and single supplement covering accommodation, meals, park and guide fee, a jeep or boat ride, and excursions at INR 4500 per person.

Reservations can be made at the Guwahati office of the company at 1st floor, Mandovi Apartments, GNB Road, Ambari,

Guwahati, 781001, Assam, India.

Telephones: +91 361 2602223/186, Fax: +91 361 2662140

email: assambengal@rediffmail.com

Web: assambengalnavigation.com

There is another newly-opened Jungle Camp besides a few cottages at Kamardwisa (Kokilabari) run by the Manas Maozigendri Eco-Tourism Society, an NGO. One can also opt for traditional home stays at Kokilabari.

For information and reservations contact: +91 9435320836.

There are a few hotels at Barpeta Road that provide comfortable accommodation at reasonable rates. The Manas Guest House (T: +91 366 260935 / 261705 / 263593) near the main market has a veg and non-veg restaurant, parking, laundry and hot water. Hotel Chitralekha (T: +91 366 260866 / 261327) is another budget hotel with 22 rooms besides a dining hall, room service and hot water. Inquiries about hotels can also be made from the Park headquarters at Barpeta Road.

SAFARIS

Both elephant and jeep safaris are available in Manas. Elephant safaris start at Bansbari and normally last one to one-and-a-half hours. However, the more adventurous can opt for a two-day safari that culminates at Kokilabari after a night's stay at Daimary. The jeep safari is usually confined to the stretch from Bansbari to Mathanguri. Rafting down the Manas from Mathanguri to Bansbari is another exciting option. With permission from the authorities, one can also venture into Royal Manas after crossing the river at Mathanguri.

BIRDING

With a total of 476 species of birds recorded (*Birds of Manas National Park* by Dr Anwaruddin Choudhury) so far, Manas can very well stake its claim to fame on the strength of its avifauna diversity alone. Of these, ten belong to the Schedule I category. These are the black-crested baza, Lagger falcon, Shahin falcon, Bengal florican, Pied hornbill, Great pied hornbill, Rufous-necked hornbill, wreathed hornbill, common peafowl and peacock pheasant.

The avian life of the whole of Manas is yet to be properly studied. Renowned ornithologist and the present president of the Bombay Natural History Society (BNHS), Asad R Rahmani, once recorded 270 species within a small study area near Bansbari in 1990.

The avian diversity of Manas accounts for 37 per cent of the total avian species found in India, which is very significant. Only Kaziranga and Corbett National Parks have more bird species than Manas. Manas also boasts of the third highest diversity of threatened birds in India after Kaziranga and Dibru-Saikhowa (also in Assam) National Parks (Islam and Rahmani 2004).

According to Dr Choudhury, in addition to the 476 listed so far, another 100 avian species may occur in Manas, some as stray or as passage migrant. There have already been reports of sightings of many of the probable species but further evidence is required to confirm their presence.

CHECKLISTS

MAMMALS

The common English names are followed by scientific names.

Monkey, lemur, etc.

* 1.   CAPPED LANGUR *Presbytes pileatus*
* 2.   GOLDEN LANGUR *Presbytes geei*
  3.   ASSAMESE MACAQUE *Macaca assumensis*
  4.   RHESUS MACAQUE *Macaca mulatta*
* 5.   SLOW LORIS *Nycticebus coucang*

Cat

* 6.   TIGER *PANTHERA tigris*
  7.   PANTHER (including black panther) *Panthera pardus*
* 8.   CLOUDED LEOPARD *Neofelis nebulosa*
* 9.   MARBLED CAT *Felis marmorata*
* 10. GOLDEN CAT *Felis temmincki*
* 11. FISHING CAT *Felis viverrina*
* 12. LEOPARD CAT *Felis bengalensis*
  13. JUNGLE CAT *Felis chaus*

Civet

  14. LARGE INDIAN CIVET *Viverra zibetha*
  15. SMALL INDIAN CIVET *Viverricula indica*
  16. COMMON PALM CIVET or TODDY CAT
       Paradoxurus ermaphroditus
  17. HIMALAYAN PALM CIVET *Paguma larvata*
* 18. BINTURONG OR BEAR-CAT *Arctictis binturong*

Mongoose

  19. COMMON MONGOOSE *Herpestes edwassdsi*
  20. SMALL INDIAN MONGOOSE *Herpestes auropunctatus*

Dog, jackal, etc.

* 21. INDIAN WILD DOG (dhole) *Cuon alpinus*
  22. JACKAL *Canis aureus*
  23. INDIAN FOX *Vulpes bengalensis*

Bear

* 24. HIMALAYAN BLACK BEAR *Selenarctos thibetanus*
* 25. SLOTH BEAR *Melursus ursinus*

Weasel

26. SMOOTH INDIAN OTTER *Lutra perspicillata*
27. COMMON OTTER *Lutra lutra*
28. YELLOW-THROATED MARTEN *Martes flavigula*
29. CHINESE FERRET BADGER *Melogale moschata*

Pangolin

* 30. CHINESE PANGOLIN *Manis pentadactyla*

Bat

31. BEARDED SHEATH-TAILED BAT *Taphozous melanopogon*
32. FULVOUS FRUIT BAT *Roussttus lescheneulu*
33. INDIAN FLYING FOX *Pteropus giganteus*
34. SHORT-NOSED FRUIT BAT *Cynopterus sphinx*
35. GREATER YELLOW BAT *Scotophilus health*

Rodent

* 36. MALAYAN GIANT SQUIRREL *Ratufa bicolor*
   37. HOARY-BELLIED HIMALAYAN SQUIRREL *Callosciurus pygerythrus*
   38. HIMALAYAN STRIPED SQUIRREL *Tamiops macclellandi*
   39. PARTI-COLOURED FLYING SQUIRREL *Hylopetes alboniger*
   40. CHINESE PORCUPINE *Hystrix brachyura*
   41. BAY BAMBOO RAT *Cannomys badius*
   42. LITTLE INDIAN FIELD MOUSE *Mus booduga*

Hare

43. RUFOUS-TAILED HARE *Kepus nrgricollis ruficaudatus*
* 44. HISPID HARE *Caprolagus hispidus*

Elephant

* 45. ASIAN ELEPHANT *Elephas maximus*

Rhinoceros

* 46. THE GREAT INDIAN ONE-HORNED RHINOCEROS *Rhinoceros unicornis*

Buffalo, wild ox, etc.

* 47. GAUR OR INDIAN BISON *Bos gaurus*
* 48. ASIATIC WATER BUFFALO *Bubalus bubalis*

Deer

49. SAMBAR *Cervus unicolour*
50. HOG DEER *Axis porcinus*
51. MUNTJAC or BARKING DEER *Muntiacus muntjac*
* 52. SWAMP DEER *Cervus duvauceli*
53. SPOTTED DEER *Axis axis*

Pig, boar, etc.

54. WILD BOAR *SUS scrofa*
* 55. PYGMY HOG *Sus salvanius*

Dolphin

* 56. GANGETIC DOLPHIN *Platanista gangetica*

* *Indicates Schedule I species under the Indian
Wildlife Protection Act-1972.*

BIRDS

Source: *Birds of Manas National Park* by **Anwaruddin Choudhury**

The following abbreviations and symbols have been used:

R = Resident
W = Winter visitor
L = Local and altitudinal migrant
M = Summer and beeding migrant
P = Passage migrant
S = Stray or Vagrant
C = Common
O = Occasional
U = Uncommon

Threat category according to BirdLife International (2004; with updates of 2006) has been given as **En**= endangered, **Cr**= critically endangered, **Vu**= vulnerable, **Nt**= near threatened, **RR** = Restricted-range.

The common English names are followed by scientific names.

Grebes

1.   LITTLE GREBE *Tachybaptus ruficollis* L U

Pelicans

2.   SPOT-BILLED PELICAN *Pelecanus philippensis* L U **Vu**

Cormorants

3.   LARGE CORMORANT, GREAT CORMORANT
       Phalacrocorax carbo   W, L C
4.   INDIAN SHAG *Phalacrocorax fuscicollis* O
5.   LITTLE CORMORANT *Phalacrocorax niger* R C

Darter

6.   ORIENTAL DARTER *Anhinga melanogaster* R C **Nt**

Herons, Egrets and Bitterns

7.   WHITE-BELLIED HERON
       Ardea insignis (=imperialis) O **En**
8.   GREY HERON *Ardea cinerea* R, L U
9.   PURPLE HERON *Ardea purpurea* L U
10.   LITTLE GREEN HERON *Butorides striatus* R C
11.   INDIAN POND HERON *Ardeola grayii* R C
12.   CATTLE EGRET *Bubulcus ibis* R C
13.   LARGE EGRET, GREAT EGRET *Casmerodius albus* L U

14. INTERMEDIATE EGRET, MEDIAN EGRET
    Mesophoyx intermedia R C

15. LITTLE EGRET *Egretta garzetta* R C

16. BLACK-CROWNED NIGHT HERON
    Nycticorax nycticorax R U

17. MALAYAN NIGHT HERON, TIGER BITTERN
    Gorsachius melanolophus R U

18. LITTLE BITTERN *Ixobrychus minutas* O

19. CHESTNUT BITTERN, CINNAMON BITTERN
    Ixobrychus cinnamomeus R C

20. YELLOW BITTERN *Ixobrychus sinensis* R C

21. BLACK BITTERN *Dupetor flavicollis* R U

Stroks

22. PAINTED STORK *Mycteria leucocephala* **Nt**

23. OPENBILL STORK, ASIAN OPENBILL
    Anastomus oscitans L U

24. WHITE-NECKED STORK, WOOLLY-NECKED STORK
    Ciconia episcopus L U

25. BLACK STORK *Ciconia nigra* W U

26. BLACK-NECKED STORK
    Ephippiorhynchus asiaticus L O **Nt**

27. GREATER ADJUTANT STORK
    Leptoptilos dubius L U **En**

28. LESSER ADJUTANT STORK
    Leptoptilos javanicus R L C **Vu**

Ibises

29. BLACK-HEADED IBIS, WHITE IBIS
    Threskiornis melanocephalus S **Nt**

Ducks and Geese

30. GREYLAG GOOSE *Anser anser* W P U

31. BARHEADED GOOSE *Anser indicus* W P U

32. LESSER WHISTLING TEAL, LESSER TREEDUCK
    Dendrocygna javanica R C

33. RUDDY SHELDUCK, BRAHMINY DUCK
    Tadorna ferruginea W C

34. NORTHERN PINTAIL, PINTAIL DUCK *Anas acuta* W C

35. COMMON TEAL, GREEN-WINGED TEAL
    Anas crecca W C

36. SPOTBILL DUCK *Anas poecilorhyncha* W, R C

36a. SPOTBILL DUCK *A. p. poecilorhyncha* W C

36b. BURMESE SPOTBILL DUCK *A. p. haringtoni* R L U

37. MALLARD *Anas platyrhynchos* W, P U

38. GADWALL *Anas strepera* W C

39. EURASIAN WIGEON *Anas penelope* W C

40. GARGANEY, BLUE-WINGED TEAL
    Anas querquedula W U

41. NORTHERN SHOVELLER *Anas clypeata* W U

42. RED-CRESTED POCHARD
    Netta (= Rhodonessa) rufina W P U

43. COMMON POCHARD *Aythya ferina* W P U

44. FERRUGINOUS DUCK *Aythya nyroca* W P U **Nt**

45. TUFTED DUCK *Aythya fuligula* W P U

46. COTTON TEAL, COTTON PIGMY GOOSE,
    QUACKY-DUCK *Nettapus coromandelianus* R L U

47. WHITE-WINGED WOOD DUCK *Cairina scutulata* R U **En**

48. GOOSANDER, COMMON MERGANSER
    Mergus merganser W C

Hawks, Kites, Eagles, Buzzards, Vultures and Harriers

49. BLACK-WINGED KITE, BLACK-SHOULDERED KITE
    Elanus caeruleus L U

50. JERDON'S BAZA *Aviceda jerdoni* R U

51. BLACK BAZA *Aviceda leuphotes* R L U

52. ORIENTAL HONEY BUZZARD *Pernis ptilorhynchus* R L U

53. PARIAH KITE, BLACK KITE *Milvus migrans govinda* L

54. BRAHMINY KITE *Haliastur Indus* O

55. NORTHERN GOSHAWK *Accipiter gentiles* W O

56. SHIKRA *Accipiter badius* R C

57. CRESTED GOSHAWK *Accipiter trivirgatus* O

58. EURASIAN SPARROWHAWK *Accipiter nisus* R L

59. BESRA SPARROWHAWK *Accipiter virgatus* R L

60. LONG-LEGGED BUZZARD *Buteo rufinus* W O
    [one record; January 2006]

61a. JAPANESE BUZZARD *Buteo buteo japonicus* W U

61b. COMMON BUZZARD *Buteo buteo* W U

62. WHITE-EYED BUZZARD *Butastur teesa* O

63. MOUNTAIN HAWK EAGLE,
    HODGSON'S HAWK EAGLE *Spizaetus nipalensis* L U

64. CHANGEABLE HAWK EAGLE *Spizaetus cirrhatus* R C

65. BONELLI'S EAGLE *Hieraaetus fasciatus* O

66. BOOTED EAGLE *Hieraaetus pennatus* O

67. RUFOUS-BELLIED HAWK EAGLE
Hieraaetus kienerii R (?) U

68. EASTERN IMPERIAL EAGLE *Aquila heliaca* O **Vu**

69. STEPPE EAGLE *Aquila nipalensis* W O

70. GREATER SPOTTED EAGLE *Aquila clanga* W U **Vu**

71. LESSER SPOTTED EAGLE *Aquila pomarina* O

72. BLACK EAGLE *Ictinaetus malayensis* L U

73. WHITE-TAILED SEA EAGLE *Haliaeetus albicilla* W O **Nt**

74. PALLAS'S FISH EAGLE *Haliaeetus leucoryphus* W U **Vu**

75. GREY-HEADED FISH EAGLE
Ichthyophaga ichthyaetus R U **Nt**

76. LESSER GREY-HEADED FISH EAGLE
Ichthyophaga humilis R U **Nt**

77. KING VULTURE, RED-HEADED VULTURE
Sarcogyps calvus R L U **Nt**

78. CINEREOUS VULTURE *Aegypius monachus* W O **Nt**

79. EURASIAN GRIFFON *Gyps fulvus* W O

80. HIMALAYAN GRIFFON *Gyps himalayensis* W U

81. SLENDER-BILLED VULTURE *Gyps tenuirostris* O **Cr**

82. WHITE-BACKED VULTURE,
WHITE-RUMPED VULTURE *Gyps bengalensis* O **Cr**

83. HEN HARRIER *Circus cyaneus* W U

84. PALLID HARRIER, PALE HARRIER
Circus macrourus W O **Nt**

85. PIED HARRIER *Circus melanoleucos* R W C

86. MARSH HARRIER *Circus aeruginosus* W U

87. SHORT-TOED EAGLE, SHORT-TOED SNAKE EAGLE
Circaetus gallicus W (?) U

88. CRESTED SERPENT EAGLE *Spilornis cheela* R C

89. OSPREY *Pandion haliaetus* W C

Falcons

90. COLLARED FALCONET *Microhierax caerulescens* R U

91. LAGGAR FALCON *Falco jugger* L U **Nt**

92. PEREGRINE FALCON *Falco peregrinus* W O

93. EURASIAN HOBBY *Falco subbuteo* W U

94. ORIENTAL HOBBY *Falco severus* R (?) U

95. RED-HEADED MERLIN, RED-NECKED FALCON
Falco chicquera L U

96. AMUR FALCON *Falco amurensis* P U

97.   LESSER KESTREL *Falco naumanni* W P O **Vu**

98.   COMMON KESTREL *Falco tinnunculus* W C

Pheasants, Partridges and Quails

99.   BLACK FRANCOLIN, BLACK PARTRIDGE
      Francolinus francolinus R C

100. SWAMP FRANCOLIN, SWAMP PARTRIDGE, KYAH
      Francolinus gularis R C **Vu**

101. BLACK-BREASTED QUAIL, RAIN QUAIL
      Coturnix coromandelica L U

102. BLUE-BREASTED QUAIL *Coturnix chinensis* R L C

103. MANIPUR BUSH-QUAIL *Perdicula manipurensis* R U **Vu**,
      RR [One record]

104. KALEEJ PHEASANT *Lophura leucomelanos* R C

105. RED JUNGLEFOWL *Gallus gallus* R C

106. GREY PEACOCK PHEASANT
      Polyplectron bicalcaratum R C

107. INDIAN PEAFOWL, COMMON PEAFOWL
      Pavo cristatus R C

Bustard-quails or Buttonquails

108. SMALL BUTTONQUAIL, LITTLE BUTTONQUAIL
      Turnix sylvatica R C

109. YELLOW-LEGGED BUTTONQUAIL *Turnix tanki* R W C

110. BARRED BUTTON QUAIL,
      COMMON BUSTARD-QUAIL
      Turnix suscitator R C

Rails and Coots

111. BLUE-BREASTED BANDED RAIL,
      SLATY-BREASTED RAIL
      Rallus (= Gallirallus) striatus R L U

112. SLATY-LEGGED BANDED CRAKE
      Rallina euryzonoides R L U

113. RUDDY CRAKE, RUDDY-BREASTED CRAKE
      Porzana fusca R C

114. BLACK-TAILED CRAKE, ELWES'S CRAKE
      Porzana bicolor R (?) U

115. BROWN CRAKE *Amaurornis akool* L U

116. WHITE-BREASTED WATERHEN
      Amaurornis phoenicurus R C

117. KORA, WATERCOCK *Gallicrex cinerea* R U

118. COMMON MOORHEN *Gallinula chloropus* R W U

119. PURPLE MOORHEN, PURPLE SWAMPHEN
Porphyrio porphyrio R C

120. COMMON COOT *Fulica atra* W U

Bustards

121. BENGAL FLORICAN *Houbaropsis (= Eupodotis)*
bengalensis R U **En**

Jacanas

122. PHEASANT-TAILED JACANA *Hydrophasianus chirurgus* L
U

123. BRONZE-WINGED JACANA *Metopidius indicus* L U

Plovers

124. NORTHERN LAPWING *Vanellus vanellus* W C

125. GREY-HEADED LAPWING *Vanellus cinereus* W C

126. RED-WATTLED LAPWING *Vanellus indicus* R C

127. RIVER LAPWING, SPUR-WINGED LAPWING
Vanellus duvauceli (=spinosus) R C

128. YELLOW-WATTLED LAPWING *Vanellus malabaricus* O

129. PACIFIC GOLDEN PLOVER,
EASTERN GOLDEN PLOVER,
Pluvialis fulva (=dominica) W C

130a. EUROPEAN LITTLE RINGED PLOVER
Charadrius dubius curonicus W,P U

130b. INDIAN LITTLE RINGED PLOVER *C.d. jerdoni* R C

131. KENTISH PLOVER *Charadrius alexandrinus* W U

132. LONG-BILLED RINGED PLOVER
Charadrius placidus W U

133. LESSER SAND PLOVER *Charadrius mongolus* W P U

Curlews, Sandpipers and Snipes

134. EURASIAN CURLEW *Numenius arquata* W P U

135. BLACK-TAILED GODWIT *Limosa limosa* W P U

136. SPOTTED REDSHANK, DUSKY REDSHANK
Tringa erythropus W U

137. COMMON REDSHANK *Tringa totanus* W P U

138. MARSH SANDPIPER, LITTLE GREENSHANK
Tringa stagnatilis W C

139. COMMON GREENSHANK *Tringa nebularia* W C

140. GREEN SANDPIPER *Tringa ochropus* W U

141. WOOD SANDPIPER *Tringa glareola* W C

142. COMMON SANDPIPER *Actitis hypoleucos* W C
143. WOOD SNIPE *Gallinago nemoricola* O **Vu**
144. PINTAIL SNIPE *Gallinago stenura* W U
145. FANTAIL SNIPE, COMMON SNIPE
    Gallinago gallinago W C
146. TEMMINCK'S STINT *Calidris temminckii* W C
147. LONG-TOED STINT *Calidris subminuta* W U

Painted Snipe

148. GREATER PAINTED SNIPE *Rostratula benghalensis* L U

Ibisbill, Stilts and Avocets

149. BLACK-WINGED STILT *Himantopus himantopus* L O
150. PIED AVOCET *Recurvirostra avocetta* W O
151. IBISBILL *Ibidorhyncha struthersii* W U

Stone Curlews, Thick-Knees

152. STONE CURLEW, EURASIAN THICK-KNEE
    Burhinus oedicnemus R U
153. GREAT STONE PLOVER, GREAT-THICK-KNEE
    Esacus recurvirostris R L U

Pratincoles or Swallow-plovers

154. ORIENTAL PRATINCOLE *Glareola maldivarum* O
155. SMALL PRATINCOLE *Glareola lactea* R,L C

Gulls and Terns

156. GREAT BLACK-HEADED GULL, PALLAS'S GULL
    Larus ichthyaetus W P U
157. BROWN-HEADED GULL *Larus brunnicephalus* W P U
158. BLACK-HEADED GULL *Larus ridibundus* W P U
159. WHISKERED TERN *Chlidonias hybridus* O
160. RIVER TERN *Sterna aurantia* R C
161. BLACK-BELLIED TERN *Sterna acuticauda* L U **Nt**

Pigeons and Doves

162. PIN-TAILED GREEN PIGEON *Treron apicauda* R L C
163. WEDGE-TAILED GREEN PIGEON *Treron sphenura* R L C
164. THICK-BILLED GREEN PIGEON *Treron curvirostra* R U
165. POMPADOUR GREEN PIGEON, GREY-FRONTED
    GREEN PIGEON *Treron pompadora* R C
166. ORANGE-BREASTED GREEN PIGEON

Treron bicincta R C

167. YELLOW-LEGGED GREEN PIGEON
     Treron phoenicoptera R C

168. GREEN IMPERIAL PIGEON *Ducula aenea* R C

169. MOUNTAIN IMPERIAL PIGEON *Ducula badia* R U

170. BLUE ROCK PIGEON *Columba livia* L U

171. BARRED CUCKOO DOVE, BAR-TAILED
     CUCKOO DOVE *Macropygia unchall* L U

172. ORIENTAL TURTLE DOVE, RUFOUS TURTLE DOVE
     Sreptopelia orientalis R C

173. EURASIAN COLLARED DOVE, RING DOVE
     Sreptopelia decaocto R C

174. RED TURTLE DOVE, COLLARED DOVE
     Streptopelia tranquebarica R C

175. SPOTTED DOVE *Streptopelia chinensis* R C

176. EMERALD DOVE *Chalcophaps indica* R C

Parakeets

177. ALEXANDRINE PARAKEET *Psittacula eupatria* R C

178. ROSE-RINGED PARAKEET *Psittacula krameri* R C

179. RED-BREASTED PARAKEET *Psittacula alexandri* R C

180. HIMALAYAN SLATY-HEADED PARAKEET
     Psittacula himalayana L U

181. INDIAN LORIKEET, VERNAL HANGING PARROT
     Loriculus vernalis R L U

Cuckoos Makohas and Coucals

182. RED-WINGED CUCKOO, CHESTNUT-WINGED
     CUCKOO *Clamator coromandus* R M U

183. PIED CRESTED CUCKOO *Clamator jacobinus* M U

184. LARGE HAWK CUCKOO
     Hierococcyx sparverioides M(?) W U

185. BRAINFEVER BIRD, COMMON HAWK CUCKOO
     Hierococcyx varius R C

186. INDIAN CUCKOO *Cuculus micropterus* R L C

187. EURASIAN CUCKOO, COMMON CUCKOO,
     KHASI HILLS CUCKOO *Cuculus canorus* M W U

188. ORIENTAL CUCKOO, HIMALAYAN CUCKOO
     Cuculus saturatus M R P U

189. LESSER CUCKOO, SMALL CUCKOO
     Cuculus poliocephalus M O

190. BANDED BAY CUCKOO *Cacomantis sonneratii* L C

191. GREY-BELLIED CUCKOO, INDIAN PLAINTIVE

CUCKOO *Cacomantis passerinus* M U

192. RUFOUS-BELLIED CUCKOO, BURMESE PLAINTIVE CUCKOO *Cacomantis merulinus* R M U

193. ASIAN EMERALD CUCKOO *Chrysococcyx maculatus* M U

194. VIOLET CUCKOO *Chrysococcyx xanthorhynchus* M U

195. DRONGO CUCKOO *Surniculus lugubris* ·R or M U

196. ASIAN KOEL *Eudynamys scolopacea* R L C

197. GREEN-BILLED MALKOHA *Phaenicophaeus tristis* R C

198. GREATER COUCAL *Centropus sinensis* R C

199. LESSER COUCAL *Centropus bengalensis* (=toulou) R C

Owls

200. BARN OWL *Tyto alba* L U

201. GRASS OWL *Tyto capensis* R (?) U
[recent record in April 2006]

202. MOUNTAIN SCOPS OWL, SPOTTED SCOPS OWL *Otus spilocephalus* L U

203. ORIENTAL SCOPS OWL *Otus sunia* R U

204. EURASIAN EAGLE OWL *Bubo bubo* R U

205. SPOT-BELLIED EAGLE OWL, FOREST EAGLE OWL *Bubo nipalensis* R U

206. BROWN FISH OWL *Ketupa zeylonensis* R U

207. TAWNY FISH OWL *Ketupa flavipes* R U

208. JUNGLE OWLET *Glaucidium radiatum* R U

209. ASIAN BARRED OWLET *Glaucidium cuculoides* R L C

210. BROWN HAWK OWL *Ninox scutulata* R C

211. SPOTTED OWLET *Athene brama* R C

Nightjars

212. GREY NIGHTJAR, INDIAN JUNGLE NIGHTJAR *Caprimulgus indicus* R C

213. LONG-TAILED NIGHTJAR *Caprimulgus macrurus* R L C

214. FRANKLIN'S NIGHTJAR, SAVANNA NIGHTJAR, ALLIED NIGHTJAR *Caprimulgus affinis* R C

Swifts

215. HIMALAYAN SWIFTLET *Collocalia brevirostris* L U

216. WHITE-THROATED NEEDLETAIL SWIFT *Hirundapus caudacutus* S

217. SILVER-BACKED NEEDLETAIL SWIFT, COCHINCHINA SPINETAIL SWIFT *Hirundapus cochinchinensis* O

218. ALPINE SWIFT *Tachymarptis melba* R L U

219. DARK-RUMPED SWIFT, KHASI HILLS SWIFT
Apus acuticauda M U **Vu**, **RR**

220. FORK-TAILED SWIFT, LARGE WHITE-RUMPED
SWIFT *Apus paciftcus* W U

221. HOUSE SWIFT *Apus affinis* R L U

222. ASIAN PALM SWIFT *Cypsiurus balasiensis* R L U

Treeswifts

223. CRESTED TREE-SWIFT, GREY-RUMPED TREE-SWIFT
Hemiprocne longipennis R U

Trogons

224. RED-HEADED TROGON *Harpactes erythrocephalus* R C

Kingfisher

225. HIMALAYAN PIED KINGFISHER,
CRESTED KINGFISHER *Megaceryle lugubris* L U

226. PIED KINGFISHER *Ceryle rudis* R C

227. BLYTH'S KINGFISHER *Alcedo hercules* R U **Nt**

228. COMMON KINGFISHER, SMALL BLUE KINGFISHER
Alcedo atthis R C

229. BLUE-EARED KINGFISHER *Alcedo meninting* R U

230. THREE-TOED FOREST KINGFISHER,
ORIENTAL DWARF KINGFISHER *Ceyx erithacus* L U

231. STORK-BILLED KINGFISHER *Halcyon capensis* R C

232. RUDDY KINGFISHER *Halcyon coromanda* M(?) U

233. WHITE-BREASTED KINGFISHER,
WHITE-THROATED KINGFISHER
Halcyon smyrnensis R C

Bee-eaters

234. CHESTNUT-HEADED BEE-EATER
Merops leschenaulti R C

235. BLUE-TAILED BEE-EATER *Merops philippinus* MC

236. GREEN BEE-EATER *Merops orientalis* R C

237. BLUE-BEARDED BEE-EATER *Nyctyornis athertoni* R C

Rollers

238. INDIAN ROLLER *Coracias benghalensis* R C

239. BROAD-BILLED ROLLER, DOLLARBIRD
Eurystomus orientalis R C

Hoopoe

240. COMMON HOOPOE *Upupa epops* R C

Hornbills

241. GREY HORNBILL *Ocyceros birostris* S
242. RUFOUS-NECKED HORNBILL *Aceros nipalensis* L U **Vu**
243. WREATHED HORNBILL *Aceros undulatus* R L C
244. ORIENTAL PIED HORNBILL, INDIAN PIED HORNBILL *Anthracoceros albirostris* R C
245. GREAT PIED HORNBILL *Buceros bicornis* R L C **Nt**

Barbets

246. GREAT HILL BARBET, GREAT BARBET *Megalaima virens* R L U
247. LINEATED BARBET *Megalaima lineata* R C
248. BLUE-THROATED BARBET *Megalaima asiatica* R C
249. BLUE-EARED BARBET *Megalaima australis* R U
250. COPPERSMITH BARBET *Megalaima haemacephala* R C

Woodpeckers

251. EURASIAN WRYNECK *Jynx torquilla* W O
252. SPECKLED PICULET *Picumnus innominatus* R U
253. RUFOUS PICULET, WHITE-BROWED PICULET *Sasia ochracea* R U
254. RUFOUS WOODPECKER *Celeus brachyurus* R C
255. LITTLE SCALY-BELLIED GREEN WOODPECKER, STREAKTHROATED WOODPECKER *Picus xanthopygaeus* R C
256. GREY-HEADED WOODPECKER, BLACK-NAPED GREEN WOODPECKER *Picus canus* R C
257. GREATER YELLOW-NAPED WOODPECKER, GREATER YELLOWNAPE *Picus flavinucha* R C
258. LESSER YELLOW-NAPED WOODPECKER, LESSER YELLOWNAPE *Picus chlorolophus* R C
259. LESSER GOLDEN-BACKED WOODPECKER, BLACK-RUMPED FLAMEBACK *Dinopium benghalense* R C
260. HIMALAYAN GOLDEN-BACKED WOODPECKER, HIMALAYAN FLAMEBACK *Dinopium shorii* R U
261. FULVOUS-BREASTED PIED WOODPECKER *Dendrocopos macei* R C
262. GREY-CAPPED PYGMY WOODPECKER,

GREY-CROWNED PYGMY WOODPECKER
Dendrocopos canicapillus R C

263. BAY WOODPECKER *Blythipicus pyrrhotis* R U

264. GREATER GOLDEN-BACKED WOODPECKER,
GREATER FLAMEBACK *Chrysocolaptes lucidus* R C

Broadbills

265. SILVER-BREASTED BROADBILL *Serilophus lunatus* R U

266. LONG-TAILED BROADBILL *Psarisomus dalhousiae* R, L U

Pittas

267. BLUE-NAPED PITTA *Pitta nipalensis* L O

268. INDIAN PITTA *Pitta brachyura* M O

269. HOODED PITTA *Pitta sordida* M U

270. BLUE PITTA *Pitta cyanea* M(?) U

Larks

271. RUFOUS-WINGED BUSH LARK,
BENGAL BUSH LARK *Mirafra assamica* R C

272. SAND LARK *Calandrella raytal* R C

273. ORIENTAL SKYLARK *Alauda gulgula* R W L C

Swallows and Martins

274. COLLARED SAND MARTIN *Riparia riparia* R L O

275. PLAIN SAND MARTIN, GREY-THROATED
SAND MARTIN *Riparia paludicola* R L C

276. BARN SWALLOW, COMMON SWALLOW
Hirundo rustica R W C

277. WIRE-TAILED SWALLOW *Hirundo smithii* S

278. RED-RUMPED SWALLOW, STRIATED SWALLOW
Hirundo daurica L U

279. NEPAL HOUSE MARTIN *Delichon nipalensis* L U

Shrikes

280. GREY-BACKED SHRIKE *Lanius tephronotus* W C

281. BLACK-HEADED SHRIKE, LONG-TAILED SHRIKE
Lanius schach W C

282. BROWN SHRIKE *Lanius cristatus* W C

Orioles

283. BLACK-NAPED ORIOLE *Oriolus chinensis* W S

284. SLENDER-BILLED ORIOLE *Oriolus tenuirostris* M U

285. BLACK-HEADED ORIOLE *Oriolus xanthornus* R C

286. MAROON ORIOLE *Oriolus traillii* R C

Drongos

287. BLACK DRONGO *Dicrurus macrocercus* R C

288. ASHY DRONGO, GREY DRONGO
Dicrurus leucophaeus R W C

289. CROW-BILLED DRONGO *Dicrurus annectans* M U

290. BRONZED DRONGO *Dicrurus aeneus* L, W C

291. LESSER RACKET-TAILED DRONGO
Dicrurus remifer R U

292. SPANGLED DRONGO, HAIR-CRESTED DRONGO
Dicrurus hottentottus R C

293. GREATER RACKET-TAILED DRONGO
Dicrurus paradiseus R C

Swallow-shrikes or Woodswallows

294. ASHY SWALLOW-SHRIKE, ASHY WOODSWALLOW
Artamus fuscus R C

Starlings and Mynas

295. SPOT-WINGED STARLING,
SPOTTED-WINGED STARE *Saroglossa spiloptera* WC

296. GREY-HEADEDMYNA,
CHESTNUT-TAILED STARLING *Sturnus malabaricus* R C

297. BRAHMINY MYNA, BLACK-HEADED MYNA
Sturnus pagodarum S

298. COMMON STARLING *Sturnus vulgaris* W S

299. PIED MYNA, ASIAN PIED STARLING
Sturnus contra R C

300. COMMON MYNA *Acridotheres tristis* R C

301. BANK MYNA *Acridotheres ginginianus* L U

302. JUNGLE MYNA *Acridotheres fuscus* R C

303. ORANGE-BILLED JUNGLE MYNA, WHITE-VENTED
MYNA, GREAT-TUFTED MYNA
Acridotheres grandis (=cinereus) L U

304. HILL MYNA *Gracula religiosa* R C

Crows, Magpies, Jays

305. COMMON GREEN MAGPIE *Cissa chinensis* R C

306. RUFOUS TREEPIE, INDIAN TREEPIE
Dendrocitta vagabunda R C

307. GREY TREEPIE, HIMALAYAN TREE PIE

Dendrocitta formosae R, LC

308. HOUSE CROW *Corvus splendens* R U

309. JUNGLE CROW, LARGE-BILLED CROW
Corvus macrorhynchos R C

Cuckoo-shrikes and Minivets

310. PIED FLYCATCHER-SHRIKE,
BAR-WINGED FLYCATCHER SHRIKE
Hemipus picatus L U

311. LARGE WOODSHRIKE *Tephrodornis gularis (=virgatus)* R C

312. COMMON WOODSHRIKE *Tephrodornis pondicerianus* R U

313. LARGE CUCKOOSHRIKE *Coracina macei* R C

314. BLACK-WINGED CUCKOOSHRIKE, SMALLER GREY
CUCKOOSHRIKE *Coracina melaschistos* L U

315. SCARLET MINIVET *Pericrocotus flammeus* R C

316. SHORT-BILLED MINIVET *Pericrocotus brevirostris* L C

317. LONG-TAILED MINIVET *Pericrocotus ethologus* L C

318. ROSY MINIVET *Pericrocotus roseus* R, L U

Fairy Bluebird, Ioras and Leafbirds

319. COMMON IORA *Aegithina tiphia* R C

320. GOLDEN-FRONTED LEAFBIRD,
GOLD-FRONTED CHLOROPSIS
Chloropsis aurifrons R C

321. ORANGE-BELLIED LEAFBIRD,
ORANGE-BELLIED CHLOROPSIS
Chloropsis hardwickii W U

322. ASIAN FAIRY BLUEBIRD *Irena puella* L U

Bulbuls

323. BLACK-CRESTED BULBUL *Pycnonotus melanicterus* R C

324. RED-WHISKERED BULBUL *Pycnonotus jocosus* R C

325. RED-VENTED BULBUL *Pycnonotus cafer* R C

326. STRIATED GREEN BULBUL *Pycnonotus striatus* W U

327. WHITE-THROATED BULBUL *Alophoixus flaveolus* R L C

328. ASHY BULBUL, YELLOW-WINGED BULBUL,
BROWN-EARED BULBUL *Hemixos flavala* W C

329. BLACK BULBUL *Hypsipetes leucocephalus* W C

Babblers

330. SPOTTED BABBLER, PUFF-THROATED BABBLER
Pellorneum ruficeps R C

331. MARSH SPOTTED BABBLER, MARSH BABBLER

Pellorneum palustre R L U **Vu, RR**

332. ABBOIT'S BABBLER *Malacocincla abbotti* R U

333. WHITE-BROWED SCIMITAR BABBLER,
     SLATY-HEADED SCIMITAR BABBLER
     Pomatorhinus schisticeps R C

334. RUFOUS-FRONTED BABBLER *Stachyris rufifrons* L U

335. GOLDEN BABBLER, GOLDEN-HEADED BABBLER
     Stachyris chrysaea L U

336. BLACK-THROATED BABBLER,
     GREY-THROATED BABBLER
     Stachyris nigriceps L U

337. STRIPED TIT BABBLER,
     YELLOW-BREASTED BABBLER
     Macronous gularis R U

338. RED-CAPPED BABBLER,
     CHESTNUT-CAPPED BABBLER
     Timalia pileata R C

339. YELLOW-EYED BABBLER *Chrysomma sinense* R C

340. JERDON'S BABBLER *Chrysomma altirostre* R U **Vu**

341. BLACK-BREASTED PARROTBILL
     Paradoxornis flavirostis R U **Vu, RR**

342. STRIATED BABBLER *Timalia earlei* R C

343. SLENDER-BILLED BABBLER
     Turdoides longirostris R U **Vu**

344. JUNGLE BABBLER *Turdoides striatus* R C

345. LESSER NECKLACED LAUGHING-THRUSH
     Garrulax monileger R C

346. GREATER NECKLACED LAUGHING-THRUSH,
     BLACK GORGETED LAUGHING-THRUSH
     Garrulax pectoralis R C

347. STRIATED LAUGHING-THRUSH *Garrulax striatus* W U

348. WHITE-CRESTED LAUGHING-THRUSH
     Garrulax leucolophus R C

349. RUFOUS-NECKED LAUGHING-THRUSH
     Garrulax ruficollis R C

350. WHITE-HEADED SHRIKE BABBLER,
     WHITE-HOODED BABBLER
     Gampsorhynchus rufulus R U

351. RED- TAILED MINLA *Minla ignotincta* W U

352. WHITE-BELLIED YUHINA *Yuhina zantholeuca* W U

Flycatchers

353. FERRUGINOUS FLYCATCHER *Muscicapa ferruginea* W U

354. RED-BREASTED FLYCATCHER,

RED-THROATED FLYCATCHER
Ficedula parva W C

355. RUFOUS-BREASTED BLUE FLYCATCHER,
SNOWY-BROWE FLYCATCHER *Ficedula hyperythra* W U

356. SLATY-BACKED FLYCATCHER, RUSTY-BREASTED
BLUE FLYCATCHER *Ficedula hodgsonii* W U

357. LITTLE PIED FLYCATCHER *Ficedula westermanni* W U

358. SLATY-BLUE FLYCATCHER *Ficedula tricolor* W U

359. LARGE NILTAVA *Niltava grandis* W U

360. SMALL NILTAVA *Niltava macgrigoriae* W U

361. RUFOUS-BELLIED NILTAVA *Niltava sundara* W U

362. PALE-CHINNED FLYCATCHER,
BROOK' S FLYCATCHER
Cyornis poliogenys W U

363. PALE BLUE FLYCATCHER *Cyornis unicolor* W U

364. BLUE- THROATED FLYCATCHER
Cyornis rubeculoides W U

365. VERDITER FLYCATCHER *Eumyias thalassina* W C

366. PYGMY BLUE FLYCATCHER *Muscicapella hodgsoni* W U

367. GREY-HEADED FLYCATCHER *Culicicapa ceylonensis* WC

368. WHITE-THROATED FANTAIL FLYCATCHER
Rhipidura albicollis R C

Monarch Flycatchers

369. ASIAN PARADISE FLYCATCHER *Terpsiphone paradisi* O

370. BLACK-NAPED MONARCH FLYCATCHER,
BLACK-NAPED MONARCH *Hypothymis azurea* R C

Warblers

371. GREY-BELLIED GROUND WARBLER,
GREY-BELLIED TESIA
Tesia cyaniventer W U

372. PALE-FOOTED BUSH WARBLER *Cettia pallidipes* R L U

373. GOLDEN-HEADED FANTAIL WARBLER,
GOLDEN-HEADED CISTICOLA *Cisticola exilis* R U

374. STREAKED FANTAIL WARBLER,
ZITTING CISTICOLA
Cisticola juncidis R C

375. GREY-BREASTED PRINIA,
ASHY-GREY WREN WARBLER
Prinia hodgsonii R C

376. PLAIN PRINIA *Prinia inornata (=subflava)* R C

377. ASHY WREN WARBLER, ASHY PRINIA
     Prinia socialis R C

378. YELLOW-BELLIED WREN-WARBLER,
     YELLOW-BELLIED PRINIA
     Prinia flaviventris R U

379. LONG-TAILED GRASS WARBLER,
     RUFOUS-VENTED PRINIA
     Prinia burnesii R U **Nt**

380. RUFOUS-RUMPED GRASS WARBLER
     Graminicola bengalensis R U **Nt**

381. COMMON TAILORBIRD *Orthotomus sutorius* R C

382. BRISTLED GRASS WARBLER, BRISTLED GRASSBIRD
     Chaetornis striatus   R U **Vu**

383. STRIATED MARSH WARBLER, STRIATED GRASSBIRD
     Megalurus palustris R C

384. THICK-BILLED WARBLER *Acrocephalus aedon* W U

385. CLAMOROUS REED WARBLER, INDIAN GREAT REED WARBLER
     Acrocephalus stentoreus W U

386. BLYTH'S REED WARBLER *Acrocephalus dumetorum* W U

387. PADDYFIELD WARBLER *Acrocephalus agricola* W U

388. BLUNT-WINGED WARBLER *Acrocephalus concinens* W U

389. TICKELL'S LEAF WARBLER *Phylloscopus affinis* W U

390. DUSKY LEAF WARBLER *Phylloscopus fuscatus* W U

391. HUME'S WARBLER *Phylloscopus humei* W U

392. YELLOW-BROWED LEAF WARBLER
     Phylloscopus inornatus W C

393. LARGE-BILLED LEAF WARBLER
     Phylloscopus magnirostris W U

394. GREENISH LEAF WARBLER *Phylloscopus trochiloides* W U

395. BLYTH'S LEAF WARBLER,
     CROWNED LEAF WARBLER
     Phylloscopus reguloides W U

396. YELLOW-VENTED LEAF WARBLER,
     BLACK-BROWED LEAF WARBLER
     Phylloscopus cantator W U **RR**

397. GOLDEN-SPECTACLED FLYCATCHER-WARBLER
     Seicercus burkii W U

398. GREY-HEADED FLYCATCHER-WARBLER
     Seicercus xanthoschistos W U

399. CHESTNUT-CROWNED FLYCATCHER-WARBLER
     Seicercus castaniceps R L U

400. YELLOW-BELLIED FLYCATCHER- WARBLER
     Abroscopus superciliaris W U

Thrushes and Chats

401. SIBERIAN RUBYTHROAT *Luscinia calliope* W O
402. BLUETHROAT *Luscinia svecica* W U
403. HIMALAYAN RUBYTHROAT *Luscinia pectoralis* W O
404. ORIENTAL MAGPIE ROBIN *Copsychus saularis* R C
405. WHITE-RUMPED SHAMA *Copsychus malabaricus* R C
406. BLACK REDSTART *Phoenicurus ochruros* W, P C
407. HODGSON'S REDSTART *Phoenicurus hodgsoni* W U
408. DAURIAN REDSTART *Phoenicurus auroreus* W C
409. PLUMBEOUS REDSTART *Rhyacornis fuliginosus* W L C
410. BLACK-BACKED FORKTAIL *Enicurus immaculatus* L U
411. SLATY-BACKED FORKTAIL *Enicurus schistaceus* L U
412. SPOTTED FORKTAIL *Enicurus maculatus* L U
413. HODGSON'S BUSHCHAT, WHITE-THROATED BUSHCHAT *Saxicola insignis* W S **Vu**
414. COLLARED BUSHCHAT, COMMON STONECHAT *Saxicola torquata* W C
415. WHITE-TAILED STONECHAT *Saxicola leucura* W U
416. JERDON'S BUSHCHAT *Saxicola jerdoni* R U
417. GREY BUSHCHAT *Saxicola ferrea* R U
418. WHITE-CAPPED REDSTART, RIVERCHAT *Chaimarrornis leucocephalus* W C
419. CHESTNUT-BELLIED ROCK THRUSH *Monticola rufiventris* W U
420. BLUE ROCK THRUSH *Monticola solitarius* W U
421. BLUE WHISTLING THRUSH *Myophonus caeruleus* R C
422. ORANGE-HEADED GROUND THRUSH *Zoothera citrina* M C
423. SCALY THRUSH, GOLDEN THRUSH *Zoothera dauma* W U
424. TICKELL'S THRUSH *Turdus unicolor* W C
425. GREY-WINGED BLACKBIRD *Turdus boulboul* W U
426. EYE-BROWED THRUSH *Turdus obscurus* W C
427. DARK-THROATED THRUSH *Turdus ruficollis* W U

Dippers

428. BROWN DIPPER *Cinclus pallasii* W O

Tits or Titmice

429. SULTAN TIT *Melanochlora sultanea* R C
430. GREY TIT, GREAT TIT *Paruts major* R C

Nuthatches and Creepers

431. CHESTNUT-BELLIED NUTHATCH *Sitta castanea* R C
432. VELVET-FRONTED NUTHATCH *Sitta frontalis* R C
433. WALLCREEPER *Tichodroma muraria* W U

Pipits and Wagtails

434. OLIVE-BACKED PIPIT, TREE PIPIT *Anthus hodgsoni* W C
435. TREE PIPIT *Anthus trivialis* W O
436. RICHARD'S PIPIT *Anthus richardi* W
437. PADDYFIELD PIPIT *Anthus rufulus* R C
438. BLYTH'S PIPIT *Anthus godlewskii* O
439. ROSY PIPIT, VINACEOUS-BREASTED PIPIT
     Anthus roseatus W U
440. FOREST WAGTAIL *Dendronanthus indicus* M O
441. YELLOW WAGTAIL *Motacilla flava* W C
442. YELLOW-HEADED WAGTAIL, CITRINE WAGTAIL
     Motacilla citreola W C
443. GREY WAGTAIL *Motacilla cinerea* W C
444. WHITE WAGTAIL, PIED WAGTAIL *Motacilla alba* W C
445. WHITE-BROWED WAGTAIL,
     LARGE PIED WAGTAIL *Motacilla maderaspatensis* L U

Flowerpeckers

446. THICK-BILLED FLOWERPECKER *Dicaeum agile* R W
447. YELLOW-VENTED FLOWERPECKER
     Dicaeum chrysorrheum L U
448. TICKELL'S FLOWERPECKER,
     PALE-BILLED FLOWERPECKER
     Dicaeum erythrorhynchos L, W U
449. PLAIN FLOWERPECKER *Dicaeum concolor* R U
450. SCARLET-BACKED FLOWERPECKER
     Dicaeum cruentatum R C

Sunbirds and Spiderhunters

451. RUBYCHEEKED SUNBIRD *Anthreptes singalensis* R C
452. PURPLE SUNBIRD *Nectarinia asiatica* R C
453. MRS GOULD'S SUNBIRD *Aethopyga gouldiae* W U

454. BLACK-THROATED SUNBIRD,
     BLACK-BREASTED SUNBIRD
     Aethopyga saturata R C

455. CRIMSON SUNBIRD, YELLOW-BACKED SUNBIRD
     Aethopyga siparaja R C

456. LITTLE SPIDERHUNTER *Arachnothera longirostra* L U

457. STREAKED SPIDERHUNTER *Arachnothera magna* W C

White-eyes

458. ORIENTAL WHITE-EYE *Zosterops palpebrosus* R C

Sparrows, Weaver and Munias

459. HOUSE SPARROW *Passer domesticus* R C

460. EURASIAN TREE SPARROW *Passer montanus* R C

461. CINNAMON TREE SPARROW, RUSSET SPARROW
     Passer rutilans W O

462. BAYA WEAVER *Ploceus philippinus* R, L C

463. BLACK-THROATED WEAVER,
     BLACK-BREASTED WEAVER
     Ploceus benghalensis R, L C

464. FINN'S WEAVER *Ploceus megarhynchus* R L U **Vu**

465. STREAKED WEAVER *Ploceus manyar* R C

466. RED MUNIA, AVADAVAT
     Estrilda (=Amandava) amandava O

467. WHITE-THROATED MUNIA, INDIAN SILVERBILL
     Lonchura malabarica O [Sen 2005]

468. WHITE-BACKED MUNIA, WHITE-RUMPED MUNIA
     Lonchura striata R C

469. SPOTTED MUNIA, SCALY-BREASTED MUNIA
     Lonchura punctulata R C

470. BLACK-HEADED MUNIA *Lonchura malacca* R U

Finches

471. COMMON ROSEFINCH, SCARLET GROSBEAK
     Carpodacus erythrinus W U

Buntings

472. CHESTNUT BUNTING *Emberiza rutila* W U

473. YELLOW-BREASTED BUNTING
     Emberiza aureola W C **Nt**

474. CHESTNUT-EARED BUNTING,
     GREY-HEADED BUNTING
     Emberiza fucata W U

475. LITTLE BUNTING *Emberiza pusilla* W C

476. CRESTED BUNTING *Melophus lathami* O

REPTILES

The common English names are followed by scientific names.

1. ASSAM WORM SNAKE *Typhlina bothriorhynchus*
2. LARGE WORM SNAKE *Typhlina diardi*
3. INDIAN PYTHON *Python molurus*
4. EARTH SNAKE *Stoliczkala khasiensis*
5. BANDED WOLF SNAKE *Lycodon fasciatus*
6. WALL'S KURI SNAKE *Oligodon melazonotus*
7. RED STRIPED KURI SNAKE *Oligodon crythrorachis*
8. FALSE WOLF SNAKE *Calamaria pavimentala*
9. IRIDESCENT SNAKE *Blythia retionlata*
10. PEAL'S WATER SNAKE *Natrix peali*
11. STRIPED KEELBACK *Amphiesma stolata*
12. GUNTHER'S KEELBACK *Amphiesma modester*
13. FALSE COBRA *Pseudoxenodon macrops*
14. GREEN KEELBACK *Macropisthodon plumbicolor*
15. CHECKERED KEELBACK WATER SNAKE *Xenochrophis piscafor*
16. ASSAM TRINKET SNAKE *Elaphe frenata*
17. BLACK BANDED TRINKET SNAKE *Elaphe porphyraceo*
18. GREEN RAT SNAKE *Zaocys nigromarginatus*
19. STRIPED SNAKE *Liopeltis frenatus*
20. ORNATE FLYING SNAKE *Chrysopelea ornate*
21. COMMON VINE SNAKE *Ahaetulla nastus*
22. LARGE SPOTTED CAT SNAKE *Bioga multimaculata*
23. ASSAM CAT SNAKE *Bioga quincunciata*
24. BANDED KRAIT *Bungarus fasciatus*
25. BINOCELLATE COBRA *Naja naja naja*
26. KING COBRA *Ophiophagus Hannah*
27. MONOCELLATE COBRA *Naja naja kaouthia*
28. BROWN SPOTTED PIT VIPER *Trimeresures mucrosquamatus*
29. GROUND MONITOR LIZARD *Varanus salvator*
30. TREE MONITOR LIZARD *Varenus spps.*
31. WATER MONITOR LIZARD *Varenus salvator*
32. GHARIAL *Gavialis gangeticus*
33. GECKO *Sphaerodactyhes spps.*

34. TURTLE *Kinosternida spps.*
35. TORTOISE *Geochelone spps.*
36. COMMON LIZARD *Calotes spps.*

ACKNOWLEDGEMENTS

Kampa Borgoary of the BTC

Abhijit Rabha of MNP

Ritesh Bhattacharya of MNP

Mohan Chandra Brahma of MNP

Assam Bengal Navigation Company,
Travel Specialists

Dr. Anwaruddin Choudhury,
Environmentalist

Aaranyak, Environmental NGO

Chandrakanta Basumatary and
Mahendra Basumatary of
Manas Maozigendri Ecotourism Society

*The author specially acknowledges his wife
Aradhana, friend Pranab Ranjan Nath, his work
colleagues, The Centre for Science and Excellence,
New Delhi, the Forest Department of Assam and
the WWF.*

NOTES

NOTES